STOLEN GIRL

STOLEN GIRL

I was an innocent schoolgirl. I was
targeted, raped and abused by a gang of
sadistic men. But that was just the beginning…
this is my terrifying true story.

Katie Taylor

with Veronica Clark

JOHN BLAKE

Published by John Blake Publishing Ltd,
3 Bramber Court, 2 Bramber Road,
London W14 9PB, England

www.johnblakepublishing.co.uk

www.facebook.com/Johnblakepub facebook
twitter.com/johnblakepub twitter

First published in paperback in 2013

ISBN: 978-1-78219-016-5

British Library Cataloguing-in-Publication Data:

A catalogue record for this book is available from the British Library.

Design by www.envydesign.co.uk

Printed in Great Britain by CPI Group (UK) Ltd

3 5 7 9 10 8 6 4

Papers used by John Blake Publishing are natural, recyclable products
made from wood grown in sustainable forests. The manufacturing processes
conform to the environmental regulations of the country of origin.

Every attempt has been made to contact the relevant copyright-holders,
but some were unobtainable. We would be grateful if the
appropriate people could contact us.

Some of the events in this book have been condensed but they are true and I am the teller of my own story. To protect the privacy of others, all names have been changed.

CONTENTS

ACKNOWLEDGEMENTS

I'd like to dedicate this book to the following people, without whom I wouldn't be the person I am today.

Firstly, I'd like to thank my dad for his tender love, care, comfort and guidance – for his loyalty and understanding. You are my friend, my hero, my father.

Also, my love goes to Kate for her warm embrace and support when things became too much to bear. I'm grateful to her for her faith in me and her hope that justice would be done – thanks to her, it was. But, most importantly, I'd like to thank her for her friendship.

I'd also like to dedicate this book to my boyfriend, who showed me what real love is. Not only has he stood by me throughout both good and bad times but he taught me how to laugh and smile again. Thank you for always making me feel so loved, wanted and safe. You are my soul mate.

To my unborn baby. I never knew you but I will never forget you. You are close in my heart every day that I live and breathe.

I think of you always. You are my guardian angel, my beautiful shining star. I'm so sorry I had to let you go. R.I.P my little angel, I love you.

To Veronica Clark, my ghost-writer, for making my dream come true in helping me to write this book. I am grateful to you for your constant encouragement, for believing in me and for always picking me up whenever life got me down.

My gratitude also goes to Allie Collins and all the team at John Blake Publishing for taking my story on and allowing me to tell it in book form. You don't know how much this means to me.

Most importantly, I'd like to dedicate this book to all those victims who are too afraid to speak out and who suffer in silence. You are not alone because I am with you every step of the way.

CHAPTER 1

FIRST STEPS

Clenching my hand into a small fist I reached up to my tip toes and knocked on the door. My brother Andrew momentarily shivered, dressed in his devil's costume.

'Trick or treat?' I asked as a middle-aged woman creaked open her front door.

'Oh my goodness, you frightened me there for a minute!' she laughed in mock-surprise, clutching a hand to her chest.

'Now what have we got here? A devil and a witch?' she guessed correctly.

I nodded and smiled up at her. I had gaps where my baby teeth had fallen out and new ones were waiting to grow through. I couldn't get used to them and, whenever I smiled, I had a habit of squishing my tongue between the empty spaces.

The woman chuckled when she saw me. 'Wait a minute, poppet. I'll just see what I've got inside for you.'

I turned to look at Dad. He was standing underneath the lamppost on the street; his hands plunged deep into the pockets of his jeans. I could tell he was freezing, but he grinned back all the same and gave me a sly thumbs-up.

Moments later the woman reappeared with a bowl of sweets.

'Take as many as you want – that's what they're there for,' she insisted.

I grabbed a handful but Andrew cheekily scooped up twice as many as me. I shot him a filthy look.

'Thank you. Bye!' we chorused as we turned to walk back up the front path towards Dad. I noticed him shiver in the cold night air.

I shivered myself and pulled my black plastic cape tight around me to try and keep in the warm, but it was no good. It was a freezing cold October night, the coldest Halloween I'd known but also the most successful. My little fingers were tightly entwined around the handles of the plastic carrier bag.

'Look how many sweets I've got,' I boasted proudly, holding my bag aloft under the amber glow of the street light.

'I've got tons more than you,' my brother sniffed, ''cos you're only a boring witch and my costume's loads better than yours!'

I stuck my tongue out at him. We were always like that; we loved one another really but we fought like cat and dog. I stuck my nose in the air as if I didn't care and continued to walk along the pavement. The night was so bitter that a silvery glaze of frost had already coated the grey path and it sparkled like glitter in the dim light. We'd been trick or treating for the last few hours and the cold, damp air had soaked through the fabric of my flimsy costume, making it feel clammy against my skin.

'Ready for home yet?' Dad asked hopefully.

I glanced back down at the carrier bag in my hand. It wasn't even full, but the bottom bit was swollen with all the sweets it

2

held inside. There were far too many – more than I could ever hope to eat but then I wondered if more treats lay ahead at the other houses. Part of me wanted to stop and go home but part of me wanted to carry on until the bag was full.

Just then a frosty breeze picked up speed and blew an icy chill down the street. Breath billowed out from my mouth like hot steam and rose up high into the night air. I noticed it and huffed a little harder. I pretended I was a scary dragon, breathing out dampened-down fire. Andrew looked over at me and tutted as if I was silly. Suddenly, I felt it. I wasn't a dragon, I wasn't even scary – I was a freezing cold little girl, I was tired and now I wanted to go home.

I stretched up and prodded Dad in the ribs.

'I'm ready to go,' I whispered, quietly enough so that my brother wouldn't hear.

Dad beckoned over to Andrew and told him it was time to go home but he was far from happy.

'There are loads more houses to go yet,' he protested, pointing down towards the end of the street, 'but now we have to turn back because of her. It's not fair!'

'Andrew,' Dad said sternly, 'stop it!'

Huffing loudly, my brother turned to follow us. I smirked at him. I'd won, for now. We headed back home with Andrew dragging his feet behind us.

The warmth from the central heating hit my face as soon as the front door of the house swung open. Mum was busy in the kitchen. As soon as she heard the door slam shut she stuck her head around the corner to greet us.

'Well, how did you get on?' she asked, holding out her arms. I instinctively ran towards her and let her envelope me in a big, warm hug. She'd been cooking and I could smell spaghetti bolognese as I buried my face into the softness of her cream jumper. Spaghetti bolognese was my favourite tea. I glanced to the side and noticed a pan of thick, red tomato sauce bubbling away furiously on top of the cooker ring.

'Look,' I said, opening up the bag. 'I got loads and loads of sweets – penny chews, refreshers, even chocolate bars!'

'Wow!' Mum exclaimed. 'You *have* been busy.'

'How about you Andrew?' she asked.

We both turned to look at my brother but his face was clouded over. He was still sulking and it was all my fault; I'd cut the evening short because I was cold.

'I got these,' he mumbled half-heartedly, showing Mum his bag of sweets, 'but I'd have got loads more if it wasn't for *her*.'

Andrew pointed his finger and pushed it hard into my shoulder.

'Ouch!' I whimpered.

'Hey, stop it you two,' said Dad, trying to intervene. 'Anyway, it doesn't matter because Mum's got a surprise for you both.'

We stopped in our tracks.

'What surprise?' I gasped.

Mum was dishing out huge reams of spaghetti. As she pulled it from the pan it slid down from the spoon onto the plates like worms. She topped off each portion with a dollop of sauce and sprinkling of cheese. Mum wiped her hands against her apron and turned to face us.

'Tonight you can eat your tea in front of the TV in the living room, because I've paid for us to watch a concert on telly.'

'What concert?' Andrew asked, his eyes darting over from Mum to me and back again.

'It's a band, they're called Steps,' she told him, 'and I think you're going to love them!'

I shrugged my shoulders; I'd never heard of a band called Steps before.

'Trust me,' said Mum. 'They sing some really good songs, very catchy, and they dance too! They're really good, Katie, you'll love them, I promise! Now grab a plate before the food gets cold and let's go and watch it.'

Minutes later we sat in front of the television as the group walked on stage. Even though there were boys and girls, they all wore the same colours, silver and black. But as soon as they started to sing and dance I could see why my mum had been so excited – they were fantastic!

Before long, I'd left most of my dinner and started munching my way through my spoils from trick or treat but I couldn't take my eyes off the screen. I was mesmerised as Steps sang and danced their way from one song to another.

'Ooh I love this one, it's my favourite!' Mum squealed as she grabbed the remote and turned the volume up so loud it slightly distorted.

The TV blared away with the volume up full blast. I was worried the neighbours might complain but Mum didn't care. Steps started to sing a song called 'Tragedy'. As soon as they said the word, the entire crowd on TV erupted in one huge cheer. Mum giggled as she dragged me up from the sofa onto my feet.

'Come on, Katie, dance with me.'

Soon we began to dance all over the front room with Mum signing in her loudest voice. I kept glancing back at the screen because I wanted to copy what Steps were doing but, however hard I tried, I kept getting the dance moves wrong.

'Don't worry,' Mum said, spinning me around in time with the music. 'I'll buy you the video then we can watch it over and over again.'

I giggled as she spun me faster and faster in her arms.

Dad chuckled as we twisted and twirled around the living room carpet. My brother Andrew huffed, rolling his eyes skyward – this definitely wasn't his idea of fun; it was far too girly. After a while, he stood up and drifted out of the room. Steps might not be his cup of tea but it opened up a whole new world to me. I was only ten years old but I'd just discovered the joy of music.

Within weeks the pretty, girly posters on my bedroom wall had been ripped down and replaced with new ones – posters of Steps. I idolised Claire and wanted to be her. She definitely had the best voice and, in my opinion, she was also the prettiest. H was my favourite boy. He was cool but not too cool; he was blond, friendly and he always smiled. I thought how nice it'd be to be friends with a boy like that.

Soon, I'd bored my best friend Lauren so much with my new-found love of Steps that she went out and bought their CD too. We became their biggest fans and would spend hours in my bedroom practising dance moves from the video Mum had bought me.

A few months later, on Christmas Day, Mum handed me a huge box. Giddy with excitement, I tore off the wrapping paper and gasped when I saw what it was – a karaoke machine.

'Thanks!' I said, running over to my parents to give them a hug.

'That's not all,' Dad smirked. He pulled out a much smaller, flatter present from behind his back. He must have been hiding it there all the time.

'Go on then, love, open it!' he urged.

I ripped off the paper and turned it over in my hands.

My eyes widened when I saw it – a Steps CD for the karaoke machine.

'Now you really can be in Steps!' Dad said and everyone laughed. It was the best day of my life.

Night after night, I played and replayed each song until I'd learned all the songs off by heart. Even though the words flashed up on screen, I didn't need to look anymore because there were all there imprinted inside my brain. Lauren practised with me and soon we knew every word and Steps dance routine.

Whenever 'Tragedy' came on, Lauren and I would jump to our feet. Whatever the song, though, I insisted on being Claire because she always seemed to have the biggest part.

Another little girl called Megan lived across the road and we roped her into being in our pretend Steps group too. We'd start by deciding who would play who and then we'd keep those parts for our entire 'performance'. But I was always Claire.

'No, Megan,' I corrected her one day in my bedroom, 'You don't do it like that, you do it like this,' I said, running through the moves a second time.

'Oh, okay…' she sighed, having another go.

'Much better now, let's take it from the top,' I said, clapping my hands as if I ran my own dance studio.

Minutes later, all three of us were standing on my bed looking across the rest of the room. The bed was our stage, we were Steps, my teddies and dolls were the audience and, in our world, they were crying out for more.

At that moment the door swung open. It was Mum; she was holding a fresh pile of folded clothes in her hands.

'Brilliant!' she cheered. She shoved the washing underneath one arm and clapped like mad.

As soon as I saw her I flushed bright red. I loved being in Steps and, when I was up on my bed – the stage – I really felt as if I really was in a pop group, but the truth was I didn't want a real audience. I was happy to perform to thousands in my imaginary world, but I didn't want to perform in the real one – I was far too shy.

'You're getting better and better every day,' Mum remarked as she closed the bedroom door behind her and went downstairs.

I looked over at Lauren and Megan; their faces were bright red too. We all felt daft and began to giggle. It was embarrassed laughter. I felt silly that we'd been caught playing Steps because that was our world – our safe little world. When I played Claire in Steps, I felt untouchable.

A few months later Mum had a surprise of her own – two tickets for a Steps concert.

'You wanna come?' she smiled, knowing full well what my answer would be.

I squealed with delight, wrapped my arms around her neck and planted a warm, sloppy kiss on her cheek.

'I can't wait!' I squealed. 'It's like a dream come true!'

Seeing my favourite band felt like the biggest night of my life and, in many ways, it was. If I wasn't already obsessed with them, after the concert I was ten times worse. I vowed to practise every night until I was as good as my heroes.

Lauren and I even made up our own dance routine to a Steps song called 'It's The Way You Make Me Feel'. By now we were so sure of ourselves that I even asked Dad to film us on his video camera. Later that day, he called us down to the living room.

'Ready?' he asked, steadying the camera in his right hand.

'Ready,' I nodded, signalling to Lauren that I would count us in.

'One, two, three…' I mouthed as Dad pressed track number four on my CD player. Within seconds music blared out from the speakers and we danced our way through the song. Afterwards, Dad pressed pause on the camera as we held our positions.

'Brilliant!' he cheered. I looked over at Lauren and we started to laugh. It *had* been brilliant and for the first time we felt it too.

I couldn't wipe the grin from my face as we rewound the film and watched it through for the first time – now we looked like proper pop stars! No one could touch us. We were protected in a perfect bubble of happiness but, as I was soon to discover, the real world was a much tougher place.

CHAPTER 2

EATING ALONE

The school was busy. Children raced around the playground in front of me at breakneck speed. I sat there wondering how I could be surrounded by so many kids, yet feel so alone. Unlike other children who played in big gangs, I only had one friend at school and that was Lauren.

Lauren and I were different in so many ways. I was a normal build with honey blonde hair whilst she was as skinny as a rake with shoulder-length dark hair. The fact we looked so different and the fact Lauren was so skinny made her a prime target for the school bullies.

'Don't walk across a grate or you'll disappear!' a boy hollered across the playground to her. I spun around to give him a nasty look but he didn't care. Lauren was the skinniest girl in school – she hated it because it made her stand out.

A few days later, one of the popular girls approached us during break time. As she wandered over towards us, she sized

Lauren up and down through beady little eyes. Her mouth sneered as she began to talk.

'We all think that you're so skinny because you can't afford to eat. Is it true? Are you too poor to buy food?'

A few girls sniggered behind her.

'Don't be stupid!' I shouted. I wanted to stick up for my friend but it was no good. Within minutes, we were surrounded by a semi-circle of jeering girls.

'Look at her, she looks like a stick!' one squealed, pointing at Lauren.

'No, she's a twig,' another laughed, 'and look, she's got two twigs for legs!'

I wrapped a protective arm around my friend's shoulder and shot them a hateful stare.

'Leave her alone!' I screamed, pulling her away.

'Ooh, we're really scared now, aren't we?' the ringleader teased, smirking at the other girls.

'Yeah,' she continued, 'we're really scared of you, Katie Taylor – you freak!'

With that they started to laugh again. Like Lauren, I was also the butt of the joke. I glanced down at my ugly black shoes and cringed. I didn't wear the right shoes, skirt or coat. Self-consciously I put my hand to my hair to smooth it down. I knew it was thick and unruly, not smooth and shiny like the other girls' hair, but I didn't want to be like them. They were girly girls, stupid and silly. Even with the right shoes, hair and coat I knew I'd never fit in. I'd never be accepted by them because they weren't very nice.

'Just ignore them, Lauren,' I insisted as I dragged her to the far end of the playground. I pulled her as far away from the hateful girls as I could. I glanced down at Lauren but it was too late. Huge tears pricked in the corner of her eyes. They swelled up into big droplets and escaped down her cheeks, dripping onto her school jumper. The knitted top soaked them up, sending the royal blue wool a darker shade of navy. Soon, a damp patch of tears had formed upon her chest.

A boy noticed Lauren's tears and came running over to finish off the job. He hovered in close but shouted out loud enough so the rest of the children could hear.

'Watch out,' he hissed, 'Here's peg legs. Hey, everybody, it's peggy legs!'

The girls were at the other end of the playground but they heard and came running over to join in. Soon more and more children had circled us. They were like sharks and now they'd seen her tears, they were going in for the kill. I clutched Lauren close as she began to sob heavily onto my shoulder.

'Peg legs! Hey, it's Peggy!'

'Peg legs, peg legs!' they chanted over and over again.

Lauren buried her head deep into my shoulder as I begged them to leave her alone. I felt utterly helpless. I wanted to stick up for her but I knew I couldn't take on the rest of the school. Instead, I just held her in my arms and told her everything would be okay. But I knew it wasn't, and it never would be. 'Peg Legs' stuck and haunted Lauren throughout her schooldays.

It was stupid because I knew Lauren, and I knew she ate more than anyone else – she was just naturally slim. There was nothing she could do.

'I'm skinny, just like Mum,' she admitted to me a few days later, the bullying still preying on her mind.

It was break time and we were bored, sat on the playground wall. I could tell by the way she spoke and bounced her heels off the brick wall that she'd thought of nothing else since.

'Mum tells me I'll be grateful for it when I'm older,' Lauren said, glancing down at her own body. 'She says I'll be slim when everyone else is fat. But I don't want to be skinny, Katie…' the words caught as a sob deep inside her throat, 'I just want to be normal.'

I looked over at my best friend and thought how tired she looked. She was tired of the constant bullying, tired of being called the same names over and over again.

'I know,' I agreed, but I didn't. Not really.

I wanted to eat dinner alongside Lauren so I could protect her from the bullies, but because I took in a packed lunch I had to eat my food in the classroom. Once, Mum had let me stay for school dinners, but when she found out I'd refused to eat anything because I didn't like the food, she wouldn't let me stay again. But Lauren stayed for school dinners, which meant she had to eat in the main hall. It left her wide open to the bullies and their cruel remarks. Every lunch time, the girls would position themselves so they could watch poor Lauren as she consumed every morsel of food. She hated them looking over at her – it made her feel self-conscious. I think they wanted to try and see what her secret was – why she didn't put on weight like everyone else. We both dreaded dinner times because we hated being apart. Despite my protests, Mum always gave me a packed lunch so I wasn't allowed in the hall with the paying kids. Instead, I'd sit alone at my desk with my sandwiches and a bag of crisps. Now and again, Mum would pop in a treat to cheer me up but it never worked because I hated being so isolated – I hated eating alone.

I wasn't the only one with a packed lunch but the other children would sit on a separate table to me. No one wanted to sit next to or be seen with me, no one other than Lauren.

EATING ALONE

Lonely and left out, I'd watch the clock, willing the next half hour to hurry up and whizz by so that I could meet my best friend in the playground. I'd watch the minute hand tick by, working its way around the clock face until it was time to leave. As soon as I could, I'd zip up my bag and run outside to be with her. Lauren was the only one who knew what it was like to be me – we understood each other. I don't know why the other girls didn't like us. They never said but they made it perfectly clear we weren't allowed in their gang. Instead, whenever we walked by they'd sneer and whisper. Then they'd fall around laughing as if sharing a secret joke, which it always was. It made me paranoid and fearful. And, without Lauren by my side, I felt even more isolated.

Sometimes, even with the nicest packed lunch in the world, I'd have no appetite. I'd watch the other kids and wonder what I'd done wrong. I never knew why they left me out, why I wasn't good enough to be part of their gang; I only knew the door was closed to me. It hurt me deeply and sometimes I'd catch a sob deep down inside my throat but I'd always refuse to let it surface. Not here, not in front of them. The bullies would never beat me. I'd never let them see me cry because I knew if I did, they'd make my life ten times worse.

Lauren and I were in different classes but we would always arrange where to meet before lunchtime so that we knew where to find one another when morning lessons were over. Usually, I was the first one there waiting by the playground wall because I was so eager to escape the loneliness of the classroom.

Lauren never meant to be late but often the queues and the chattering children would hold her up. I hated sitting around because, apart from a solitary skipping rope, everything in the playground needed more than one person. Games always involved a group of kids. Instead, I'd sit there forlornly, waiting for my friend, trying not to catch anyone's eye in case they turned on me.

Even though she'd often be late, I didn't mind because as soon as I saw her running out of the school hall my face would light up. Once outside we'd run off together into a far corner, where no one would find us. Then we'd be back — safe in our imaginary world, where I was Claire and she was Lisa. We were Steps and no matter how mean the bullies were, we didn't care because together we'd sing and conquer the world! However, first I had to conquer my times tables. Maths was my worst subject. I knew it and so did the teacher, but most of all, so did all the other children.

'Hey, dumbo, why didn't you know that one? It was easy!' A boy shouted across the class at me one day when I got a simple question wrong. The others soon joined in.

'Idiot!' another mouthed in my direction.

'No,' a girl hissed, 'she's as thick as pig shit!'

I tried to hide at the back of the classroom hoping the teacher wouldn't notice me. I convinced myself if I hunched my shoulders and kept my head down then maybe I could make myself invisible. If she couldn't see me then she wouldn't be able to pick me out to ask me anything, but she always did.

One day she asked me the answer to a simple maths question but I didn't have a clue.

'Katie, I asked what is eight times eight?' The teacher tapped her fingers impatiently on my desk, waiting for an answer.

Suddenly, my heart beat furiously and my mouth went bone dry. The middle of my palms pricked with perspiration and I felt clammy with sweat as I tried to think of something, *anything* to say. But the harder I thought, the more my mind went blank. By now, all eyes were on me. I felt them burning into me, all waiting for an answer I didn't have. My head felt light and dizzy as the room began to spin. Everyone was watching me. I saw them but at the same time, I saw no one, only the teacher standing there, waiting. But I didn't know my times table. I didn't have a clue what eight times eight was. Maybe I could just say a random number and make her go away? For a split second I considered it. A random number came into my head but what if it was too high or too low? Then I'd look even more stupid; the teacher would know that I'd guessed and I'd be in even worse trouble.

'Err…err…' I stuttered, trying to think of something to say.

The classroom was silent except for my fumbling voice. The teacher waited. I looked either side in the faint hope that someone might help me and whisper the answer. But I knew they wouldn't because I didn't have any friends here. Lauren was my only friend and she was in another class – I was on my own.

'Katie, I'm waiting,' the teacher said, still tapping her fingers. I squirmed under her gaze. By now sweat was prickling across my forehead. I desperately searched her eyes in the hope that I might be able to read the answer from them but it was useless. *I* was useless. I didn't have a clue and everyone knew it. My silence made the other children restless. I heard stifled giggles in front of me and felt my face begin to flush red. I was stupid and now everyone knew.

'Loser,' a boy called out from the back of the class. The teacher pretended not to hear him, which made the others call out even more.

'Dumbass,' one boy scoffed.

'She's doesn't know, Miss, 'cos she's thick!' a girl hollered

17

from the other side of the room. They laughed out loud. My face felt red hot as I burned with shame, but the redder I became, the more they laughed.

'Look, her head looks like a beetroot. She's a thick beetroot!' a boy chipped in. By now the whole class was in an uproar.

'Shush, be quiet!' the teacher scolded. But the damage had already been done. They'd seen it. They all knew I couldn't do maths and now they'd make it their business to chip away at what little confidence I had left.

'I bet she doesn't even know what one plus one is,' a girl hissed sarcastically, loud enough for me to hear, as I packed my books after the lesson had finished.

'Yes I do!' I insisted, but the girl wasn't listening anymore, she'd turned away and was giggling with her friends. I never felt so alone in my life.

'She's dumb,' the girl said, momentarily turning back to face me. 'I think we should call her Dumbo or something. Dumbo or Thicko!'

'Yes,' said another, 'from now on we'll call her Dumbo!'

I didn't know what I'd done to make them so angry and nasty towards me. Whatever it was, I decided that if I couldn't be good at maths then I'd try my best at everything else. Thankfully, I loved English and discovered that I had a natural talent for it. At home, I was a real bookworm. Mum and Dad were always buying me books and would encourage me to read as much as I could. I read so much that my head was bursting with ideas of my own and my nose was never out of a story. When I read, it helped me escape my own world and become part of another inside the story. The more reading I did, the better I became at writing my own stories in school.

'Very good, excellent in fact. Well done, Katie,' the teacher said one day as she placed my exercise book back on the desk in front of me. My heart was in my mouth as I flicked open my homework page. I'd spent ages on this story and I'd hoped for a good mark. As soon as I saw the 'A' at the bottom of the page in red ink, I felt so happy I thought my heart would burst. But the other kids weren't quite so impressed.

'Look at her,' one girl said to another at the desk behind me. 'She thinks she's it just because she's teacher's pet.' They'd both noticed the 'A' in my English book.

I ignored her. She was only jealous because I'd found something I was good at, something I enjoyed doing. But the higher my grades in English, the more the bullying intensified. I'd been Dumbo in maths, yet here in the English class I was called 'swot'. I was a 'Goody Two-Shoes', even a 'saddo', for getting things right.

'Clever cow,' one girl sniffed at the end of the lesson one day.

'Yeah,' her mate chipped in. 'You're well gay, writing stories.'

Both girls knocked into me as they barged past. I couldn't believe it. I was in a no-win situation. I was either too thick or too clever; whatever I did, I just couldn't seem to get it right. I couldn't make these kids like me. I was different to them in more ways than one and they saw it in me. They didn't like the fact that I wasn't a girly girl. I didn't have the latest shoes, skirt or bag and I stood out because of it. I took a packed lunch when most kids stayed for dinner, I was rubbish at maths but too clever at English. They didn't like me and, whatever I did, there was nothing I could do that would ever change their minds.

CHAPTER 3

THE CHRISTMAS PARTY

I was still only eleven years old when I started my periods. I didn't even know what a period was and so, when I saw the toilet bowl full of blood, I panicked and went running straight to Mum. I was so scared that I didn't even stop to flush the loo first.

Bleary-eyed, my brother Andrew stumbled into the bathroom for a wee and reeled back in horror.

'Mum! Katie's left blood all in the toilet – I think she's bleeding to death!' he screamed in horror. His voice was so loud it carried throughout the house. It was a warm day and the windows were wide open. I cringed because I was worried everyone would hear, even the neighbours.

Mum was shocked when she heard him call. Then she saw my face, tear-stained and frightened. I didn't understand what was happening to me and at first I was scared I was dying. Mum was upset too. Upset she was losing her little girl to puberty so early. I didn't realise it then but that day I'd taken my first steps towards becoming a woman.

'Does it hurt anywhere?' Mum said, gently rocking me in her arms. I smelt her perfume, stale from the night before, and immediately felt reassured. I clutched a hand around my stomach; it felt both hard and swollen. I winced as it twisted inside with pain.

'My tummy hurts,' I whispered.

Mum pulled me close again and smoothed my hair beneath the palm of her hand.

'It's called a period, Katie. Women have them once every month, it's just something that happens – it's nothing to be frightened of.'

I looked at Mum with wide eyes.

'Every month? You mean I'll have to go through this *every* month?' I gasped. Mum looked down at my confused face and nodded.

I shuddered at the thought of so much pain. 'Will it hurt like this every time?'

'Sometimes it will hurt more than others but the first time is always the worst. After a while you'll get used to it, I promise.'

With that she got up, walked over to a side cabinet and pulled open the top drawer. I knew it contained her underwear but she pushed it to one side and pulled something out. Holding it in her hand, she turned to face me.

'You need to use these, Katie,' she explained, waving some white things in the air. 'They're called sanitary towels and they'll stop the blood from getting on your clothes.'

I wanted to weep. I'd always been in such a rush to grow up but now it'd happened, I just wanted to be a little girl again.

Andrew's voice carried across the landing.

'Yuck, this is horrible! What should I do? Flush it away?' he called.

'Yes, Andrew,' she replied. 'Just flush the toilet, please.'

After that, Mum always made sure I carried a sanitary towel in my school bag just in case. I didn't tell anyone in my class that I'd started my periods. But every time I needed to go to the toilet, they'd all watch and wait for me to pull the odd white thing from my bag. The teacher would nod, as if it was a secret between us. Inwardly, I'd cringe and try to hide the sanitary towel. I'd fold it, cover it with my hands, even push it up inside my sleeve, but my crimson face gave me away. I waited for the name-calling but to my astonishment, nothing was ever said. If the other girls were curious, they never asked. Maybe they felt young in comparison with me, I don't know. But whatever it was, my periods, like everything else in my life, separated me from the other girls in my class – the gulf between us growing wider every day.

Eventually, I confided in Lauren. She confessed that she'd not yet started her periods and that she felt jealous that I had.

'My boobs haven't grown either,' she moaned, peeking down her school shirt. 'I'm as flat as an ironing board!'

I shook my head.

'Lauren, honestly, you don't want to start your periods. They're horrible and they really hurt.'

But my best friend just shrugged and looked off into the distance. She was in a hurry to grow up and I knew that I wouldn't convince her otherwise. Suddenly I remembered the nasty girls.

'You won't tell anyone, will you?' I begged, clutching her arm.

'Don't be daft, of course I won't.'

I thought the others probably already knew but I fretted that if Lauren said something, they'd make an even bigger thing out of it. However, true to her word, my best friend never told a soul.

A few weeks later, the music teacher announced there was to be a school play and there would be auditions for a song and dance routine. To my horror, Lauren got it into her head that we should audition for the parts.

'You're joking, right?' I asked, my mouth hanging wide-open with shock. Peg Legs and Dumbo in the school play? I thought she'd gone mad!

'Why not?' Lauren exclaimed, throwing her hands up in the air in frustration. 'Why not us, Katie?'

I shook my head in disbelief.

'No way,' I told her. Only the cool popular kids got to be in something like this. Only the popular kids ever got to perform in the school play, it was an unwritten rule. However, Lauren was adamant.

'But we're good,' she insisted. 'Everyone who's ever seen us says so.'

Deep down I knew she was right but it went against every-thing we'd ever been told by the bullies. I was always trying to make myself invisible; doing everything I could to stay out of the limelight but now Lauren wanted to put us up on the stage! Surely it'd give them even more ammunition to fire at us.

But Lauren was my best and only friend, and she really wanted to do this. We'd always stuck together. I couldn't let her go in alone, so in the end we both went.

The main hall was packed when we walked in through the door. Sure enough, all the popular girls were there and they gasped as soon as they saw us. Strangely, Lauren seemed excited and not in the least bit nervous but I was so scared that my legs felt like jelly, as though they might collapse underneath me.

As soon as they saw us sneak into the room they began to nudge one another. But Lauren was adamant we'd do this. She tugged at my sleeve and pulled me over towards the piano, where the music teacher was sitting.

I could still hear them whispering as we plonked ourselves down on comfy chairs. Lauren didn't seem to mind that everyone was looking over but it bothered me. I glanced out through the window of the hall into the school playground. I wished I was outside, running free and as far away from there as possible. Deep down I knew we'd be safe in the audition – the music teacher was strict and wouldn't stand for any nonsense. It was afterwards, in the playground, that we needed to worry.

One by one, each group was called out to sing the same song, one called 'Moonlight', which I'd never heard before. It was a slow song and we had to listen to it a few times before she handed us each a sheet of lyrics.

There were ten girls auditioning for a part. Eight of them were from the popular set; only two weren't –Lauren and me. But the teacher hadn't finished. There were only four parts up for grabs so we'd have to compete against each other for a place. The nasty girls smirked at us as if it was already in the bag. I cringed because I knew that we didn't stand a chance.

But as soon as Lauren and I started to sing I forgot all about the girls. Instead, it was just us two in that room. Suddenly, I was in my bedroom, back in my safe imaginary world. We were up on stage and no one could touch us. I shut my eyes and lost myself in the song. Normally, apart from Lauren, I'd never sing in front of anyone, yet here I was, hitting every note. My voice lifted up, filling the hall. When I sang, I felt free. It was only once we'd reached the end that I dared open my eyes. I expected laughter, a sly comment, but there was nothing. Instead the popular girls sat there open-mouthed with shock. A warm feeling of satisfaction rose up inside me; that had shut them up.

Lauren nudged me with her elbow and quivered with excitement, as if she knew that we'd just done something very special.

Soon the audition was at an end. The teacher told us to keep the song lyrics so that we could all practise at home. But I didn't need them. The words were already inside my head, held in that one special moment I would savour forever — the day I wiped the smiles off the bullies' faces.

Still, Lauren and I practised like mad. We sang at each other's houses, honing every note until it was perfect. We even worked out simple harmonies to make the song sound better. Although we loved every minute, I convinced myself that's all it was — just a bit of fun. There was no way that we'd ever be chosen. However, we were one step ahead of the rest of them because by now, we knew the lyrics off by heart; we didn't need song sheets.

After a few weeks, the music teacher asked each girl to sing a verse solo. My heart began to thud. My head swam with fear as each girl sang before. I wondered what to do — I was terrified that they'd laugh at me, that they'd ruin the one thing that made me truly happy. But, before I knew it, the music teacher had called out my name.

'Katie, are you ready?'

I nodded my head. The worst they could do was laugh but

I was used to that. I took a deep breath and began. As the words left my mouth, I noticed the teacher nodding at me with approval. It spurred me on and gave me confidence until I'd sung the entire first verse solo in front of them all. When I finished, I glanced down at my feet, waiting for the laughter, but none came. Instead there was a deafening silence. Lauren looked over at me and gave me a quick thumbs-up: I'd done okay.

Moments later the music teacher called out the names of the four chosen girls. My heart sank when I heard her call two of the popular girls. They squealed with excitement and hugged one another as though it'd been expected. The others waited but they weren't called. As soon as I heard mine and Lauren's names, I jumped for joy and punched the air. I couldn't believe it. Gripping Lauren's hand I gave it a reassuring squeeze. For once, we'd come out on top – we were better than them.

Of course they weren't happy but I didn't care. There was nothing they could do, even if they stood there forever, calling us all the names under the sun, it wouldn't change a thing. We'd won this on our own merit. We were finally up on stage and this time it was for real. The dance routine needed to be performed in pairs, so Lauren and I naturally teamed up. During rehearsals we felt on top of the world. It wasn't a huge stage like the arena where I'd seen Steps, but it didn't matter – we were there because we were the best. We practiced and practised until our feet ached. Even though we'd totally mastered the dance routine, we continued to practise – we were determined to show them all we deserved to be there.

When the night finally arrived, my hands shook as I pulled on my black trousers and silver glittery top. Lauren called for me and we walked to school. We were laughing and joking, dizzy with happiness because we were about to perform for real. But as I saw the school in the distance, the butterflies rose inside my stomach.

We sat backstage and, as the minutes ticked by, I became more and more nervous. The hall was packed. Kids from the school, parents and teachers were all crammed in waiting for the big moment. Suddenly, I heard a round of applause – it was our cue to go on. Lauren and I strode onto the stage, our heads held high as we took our positions. The lights were bright but as I looked out into the distance I noticed a couple of hands waving at me. It was Mum and Dad – they looked so proud. They were here to witness the biggest moment of my life and I prayed that I wouldn't mess up. The heat from the spotlight seared my skin, its bright light almost blinded me but as soon as the piano started up and familiar notes filled the hall, I forgot my nerves. Lauren and I sang our hearts out. We felt amazing; it was our moment. To be watched. To be seen. To be heard. And not a soul laughed. No one.

In that one moment, the kids could see, if only for a few minutes, that we weren't just Peg Legs and Dumbo. We were just like them – normal kids with a love and passion for music. Up on that stage, we felt like superstars because we'd been the best – we'd been chosen.

At the end of the routine, the whole hall erupted with applause. Lauren gave my hand a final squeeze as we stepped forward with the other girls and took a bow. Just for that one night, we were untouchable. We were someone – we were better than the bullies simply for being ourselves, and it felt fantastic. However, the best night of my life only fuelled their anger. They despised us for it because that night we'd blurred the boundaries. Being on stage was their territory, not ours.

We'd stood up to them but at the same time we stood out because of it. Then something else happened to make things even worse.

My body was rapidly changing. All the other girls were flat-chested but now when I pulled on my school jumper I noticed it was tighter because I was beginning to grow breasts. I was maturing in more ways than one. My hips and bum began to fill out; I became curvy and I looked as though I had grown up almost overnight. When I stood next to Lauren, we looked ridiculous. I was changing but Lauren was still trapped in the body of a child. By hanging around together we emphasised everything we felt self-conscious of. I seemed to make Lauren look even skinner; she made me look older. I hated being different from my friend and despised my body.

I was developing at such a rate that Mum decided it was time to buy me my first bra and, despite my apprehension, when I first put it on it made me feel older and wiser than the other girls. I knew I was the only one to wear a bra but I was too frightened to let them see it. Instead, when everyone else got changed in the communal dressing room, I'd sneak off and change behind a locked toilet door.

The school had a Christmas disco planned for all the pupils. Lauren and I had been looking forward to it for weeks. We practised our Steps dance moves so that we'd be extra-good on the night. I was convinced that we'd wow the other kids and that, when they saw how talented we were, the bullies would leave us alone, and maybe they'd even want to be our friends.

I pestered Mum for a new outfit and finally she buckled under the pressure. After hours trawling the shops I found the perfect clothes – a pair of black jeans with cool splits at the ankles and a glittery gold disco top with a big red heart on the front. As soon as I looked at myself in the changing-room mirror I knew it was perfect. I looked grown-up but I also looked trendy. For the first time in my life I felt as if I belonged. As I studied my reflection, I thought this outfit would change everything – it would make me fit in with the popular girls. But I couldn't have been more wrong.

On the day of the disco Lauren knocked on my front door.

'Wow!' she gasped as I opened it to find her standing there on the doorstep.

'Do you like it?' I asked, posing awkwardly in the doorway. I still felt a little unsure of myself but gave her a self-conscious twirl all the same.

'*Like* it? I love it! You look ace, Katie. Really pretty.' Lauren insisted.

I hugged her gratefully – she'd just made me feel like a million dollars.

'You look lovely too,' I said as I grabbed my coat and off we set down the road towards the school.

We could hear the music even before we'd even reached the main entrance. The hall was hot and sweaty with too many kids running around and not enough windows open.

'God, it's like an oven in here!' I shouted to Lauren over the boom of the music.

She nodded and wafted her hand against her face to create a draft. It was boiling.

Disco lights flashed and lit up the room with neon colours. We threw our coats on a pile in a cloakroom and headed towards the dance floor. As we did so I spotted the usual group of popular girls standing in a corner of the room. I wanted to smile over but I knew it was pointless. Maybe now they'd seen my new outfit they'd be a little kinder. However, the more I looked over, the more I noticed something was wrong. They were standing there, pointing towards us, whispering. Lauren and I started to dance but I couldn't shake off the uneasy feeling. They were looking over and talking about us but I didn't know why. I saw one girl dip her head and say something to the rest of the group; they all nodded and began to laugh.

I glanced down at my top, I wondered if I'd spilt toothpaste or something down it, but there was nothing there. I was worried. Why were the girls looking over and what was so funny? My eyes darted from the group back to Lauren. She'd spotted them too but was just as baffled as me. I fretted; maybe we were dancing wrong? It was hopeless, I felt stupid. I was just about to suggest we sit down when the ringleader approached. Her name was Melanie and she was a nasty piece of work. She was pretty and she knew it. I hated her with a passion. The others pushed her over towards us, egging her on to say something. I waited to see what was wrong. Halfway across the dance floor she stopped and momentarily turned back to face the group. As she did, everyone started to laugh. They were so loud that you could hear them over the din of the music.

More and more kids joined in the group so they could share the joke. It was as if half the hall were standing in the corner, whispering and pointing over.

I'd gone to the disco feeling a million dollars but now I felt less than worthless. I wanted the ground to open up and swallow me whole. The girl smirked as she approached, but she wasn't smirking at Lauren, she was smirking at me. My heart sank; I knew whatever it was she had to say, her words would crush me.

She looked me up and down for what seemed like an eternity before she finally spoke.

'Everyone here thinks you've got tissues stuffed down your top.' she said, pointing at my chest.

I self-consciously pulled my top away from my body. The girl saw me do it and turned back to the group, who dissolved into fits of laughter. Suddenly my trainer bra felt too tight against my chest. My heart thumped hard with both fear and embarrassment.

'What?' I asked, even though I'd heard her the first time.

'I *said*,' she began to shout, her voice was so loud that others nearby could hear, 'we all think you've got tissues stuffed down your top and *they*,' she said, pointing towards my breasts, 'aren't real.'

I was mortified. I wanted to die right there and then but the horror on my face only made them roar even more. I glanced at the group and then down at the floor. I felt utterly humiliated – the whole school was laughing at me. Even Lauren didn't know what to say. We both just stood there.

'But…but…I *don't* use tissues,' I stammered, trying to find the right words.

'Well, we think you do and it looks stupid. You look like a slag!' Melanie said, turning on her heel. With that, she headed back to the safety of the group. Her words hit me like a right hook to the side of my face. By now the whole room was in on the joke and everyone was looking over, pointing and laughing. Tears pricked at the back of my eyes – I could feel them coming and I didn't want anyone to see, so instinctively I ran for the door. I heard Lauren's voice calling me but I didn't turn back. Instead I kept on running. I couldn't stay, not after that. I ran and ran until I saw the lights of our front room. I sneaked in quietly through the back door and went straight up to my bedroom and closed the door behind me. Burying my head deep into the pillow, I sobbed my heart out. I listened out for Mum, but she was in the front room and hadn't heard me come in. I was glad – I didn't want to tell her what they said to me and how miserable my life was at school. It felt more and more like a prison each day.

I never told Mum a thing – I was too embarrassed. Instead, I pulled off the stupid top and threw it in the bin. I'd loved that top – it had made me feel special and part of the gang – but now I wanted to shred it into tiny pieces because it was a reminder that I was nothing like them and I never would be.

The girls had been right all along: I was different. But what I didn't realise then was that it was this that'd mark me out in more ways than one – it would be this which would separate me from my best friend forever.

CHAPTER 4

THE GIRL WITH THE GOLDEN HAIR

As puberty really began to kick in, so my shape continued to change. I hated it because I looked so different compared to my classmates.

Soon hormones were taking over and it wasn't long before my honey-blonde hair began to dull to a horrible mousey-brown colour. I didn't care but Mum wasn't keen and she bought a special spray-in lotion to give my hair a 'natural sun-kissed look'. Unfortunately, it did nothing of the sort. Instead of making me look like I'd been kissed by the rays of the sun, all the spray did was wreck my hair, turning it both the colour and texture of yellow straw. Still, Mum persevered. Perhaps she thought if I was blonde then I'd become more popular at school but she was wrong. The yellower my hair became, the more the bullying intensified. Soon, my usual nickname of Dumbo changed to 'Mophead'. When my dark roots reappeared at the end of each month they produced a thicker, darker stripe at my crown and the name-calling upped to another level.

'Watch out, here comes Mophead!' the popular girls would jeer every time I walked by.

I begged Mum not to spray the awful stuff in my hair but she thought she was doing me a favour.

I started at secondary and the nickname followed me across town and to my new school. Of course, the other children from the different intake schools took great pleasure in joining in and shouting it out on every occasion. I think they were relieved I was the target and not them.

'Is it a bird? Is it a plane? No, it's Moppy Taylor!' They'd all chant in unison, until the only person not laughing was me.

Luckily, the girl who lived across the road from me and my former imaginary Steps band member, Megan, went to the same secondary school and so did Lauren. As luck would have it, Megan and I ended up in the same form group together. I sat close to Lauren that first morning, waiting for my name to be called out, praying they'd put us together, but it wasn't to be. Instead, Megan's name was called and we both had to leave Lauren to her own fate. When we met later that day at break, Lauren told us how she'd been put in a class on her own with all the primary school bullies.

'Don't worry,' I reassured her. 'We'll still meet up every break and lunchtime, won't we, Megan?' I glanced over at my new friend, who nodded in confirmation.

But I'm ashamed to say I was just relieved it was Lauren and not me who'd been thrown into the lions' den. Poor Lauren, I felt so guilty – she was on her own, but at the same time, I was grateful it wasn't me because life was hard enough.

Having Megan in my form class helped a little but she was

as meek and mild as I was, so we didn't stand a chance against the others. Megan would try her best to stand up for me, often putting herself in the line of fire.

'Shut up,' she hollered one day, shouting the bullies down. They'd been saying my hair looked like a wig. 'It's not a wig, it's Katie's own hair!' Then, as if to prove the point, she pulled at it to show it was still attached to my head.

It hurt when she tugged but I didn't cry out. She needed to do it to get them off my back but they wouldn't stop. I refused to cry – I wouldn't let them see they'd beaten me. But my voice gave me away because when they stole my confidence, they stole my voice too. Now it was barely a whisper; I hid at the back of the class and refused to put my hand up even when I knew the answer. I was running scared.

One day, I trudged sadly along the corridor to maths. I didn't even have Megan, because she was in a higher group. Wearily, I made my way to the back of the class out of the way of the teacher.

'Katie Taylor, not there,' he called. He was standing up and looking directly at me. 'I want you at the front, where I can see you.'

He pointed towards an empty chair at the front of the room.

My face flushed as the class began to whisper. I gathered up my things but was in such a fluster that I dropped my pencil case. It was already unzipped and, as it hit the ground, dozens of pens and pencils spilled out across the floor.

The teacher sighed and rolled his eyes as if he'd given up on me too. It was a green light for nasty comments as I scrambled around on the ground.

'Look,' said an ugly freckled-face boy, 'Mophead's dropped her pencils.'

'Yeah,' agreed a scrawny-looking boy next to him, 'she's so dumb she can't even pick them up.'

The whole class laughed.

But things were about to become even worse. The more I tried to get out of answering questions, the more my teacher noticed. One day, at the end of the lesson, he strode over to my desk. The rest of the class looked up from their books and tried to earwig what he was saying.

'Katie, I think you might need a little bit of help during lessons, so I'm going to ask Mrs Wright to come in and help you from now on. Is that okay?'

I went bright red and heard a girl snort behind me. I felt so ashamed that a part of me died inside.

Mrs Wright, the teaching support assistant, was useless. She had no control over the children because no one would listen to her. How on earth was a woman like that ever going to help me?

The following week I prayed for the earth to swallow me up when I spotted her slipping into the room. Her eyes scanned the class and when she met my gaze, she raised a hand in acknowledgement. I shifted uneasily in my seat as the others nudged and whispered to one another.

'I'm here to help Katie Taylor with her maths skills,' she repeated, in case anyone didn't already know.

'Ah yes,' the maths teacher replied. 'She's just over there.' He gestured over towards me.

'Katie, get up and fetch a chair from the back of the class for Mrs Wright, so she can help you.'

I felt my whole body crumple. Maths was excruciating enough without having an extra teacher to point out how stupid I really was. The nudges and whispers continued as I made my way to the back of the classroom and grabbed a chair. I tried not to look at anyone but try as I might, I couldn't help but notice some of the popular girls pulling faces. Holding the chair aloft, I turned my head back towards them and stuck out my tongue. Why did they have to make me feel so utterly useless?

After that day, whenever I had a maths lesson, Mrs Wright would be by my side. The woman had the patience of a saint but every time she pointed out a simple mistake I wanted to die on the spot because she'd repeat it loud enough for everyone to hear.

'No, Katie, you need to add five and 105 together then divide it by that number...' she said, pointing down at the page in my book. I didn't need to look up to know that the whole class was laughing. I was still on the simple stuff; they were way ahead of me now.

One day, when the maths teacher was out of the room, the other kids started on me. Even though Mrs Wright was sat by my side, they just ignored her. Instead, a freckle-faced boy sauntered over and asked if he could borrow a pen.

'No,' I replied curtly. 'Go away.'

But he wasn't giving up.

'Come on, Mophead, lend us a pen,' he taunted. He looked back at the rest of the class, who began to laugh.

'Don't be tight. I bet you've got loads in there, let me have a look,' he said, grabbing my pencil case up off the desk.

'Give it back,' I demanded, but he ignored me.

'God, Moppy's got tons of posh pens in here! Hey, who wants one?'

A load of hands shot up into the air.

I looked at Mrs Wright for support. I waited for her to say

or do something but instead she just sat there. Then she did something that stole my breath – she turned away. The boy saw it. He knew he'd won – he was in charge here now.

'Hey, who wants a pen?' he said, throwing the pencil case across the classroom. It sailed high above the heads of the other children and came crashing to the ground with a thud.

'Don't,' I called, 'you'll break them.'

I looked to Mrs Wright but she refused to get involved. My heart sank – I was on my own.

'Ooh, don't break Mophead's precious pens now!' the boy mimicked in a high-pitched voice. It made everyone giggle.

Someone picked up the pencil case and threw it again. It happened over and over. I tried to catch it but it was useless by now, the whole class was in on it.

'Urrghh!' one of the popular girls shrieked, 'don't throw it to me!' She pushed the pencil case off her desk in disgust. 'I might catch something.'

Tears pricked behind my eyes. No one cared about my stuff – it was disposable, just like me. To everyone else they were only pens but to me they were special because my mum had bought them. She knew how much I loved writing so she'd got some fancy pens to encourage me. But no one cared about me or my feelings, not even the teacher.

Wearily, I flopped down into my plastic chair and waited for them to tire of their silly game. But the pencil case continued to fly through the air. I looked to the support teacher, tears brimming in my eyes, but she wouldn't even look at me. She wasn't going to help; no one was. This was my life now – I was a target for everyone to poke fun at.

I didn't fit in here and I never would. It was a different school – a new start – but I still wore the wrong shoes. My trousers were too tight and I carried my books in a backpack instead of a girly shoulder bag. I wasn't into fashion and it showed. Part of me wanted to fit in but another part didn't because deep down, I didn't want to be like them: I knew they were shallow and horrible.

Mum continued to spray my hair and it soon became so frazzled that even she agreed something had to be done.

'We're going to the hairdresser,' she announced one night after school. 'We need to sort out your hair.'

I looked at my reflection in the bathroom mirror. Was I really that repulsive and stupid? I didn't know anymore. The bullies had chipped away what little confidence I had left.

My hair looked dry and coarse and I tried to pull my fingers through it, but every time I did, they just snagged the ends. It was so brittle, it was beginning to snap off. Mum was right, something had to be done.

The following day was a Saturday, so we caught the bus into town and walked into a nearby hair salon. The shop was packed and suddenly I felt very conscious of my straw-yellow hair. It looked as if I'd poured a bucket of custard over my head.

A young girl approached us breezily. She looked at me and tried not to laugh – it was obvious she'd seen it all before.

'I need to speak to someone,' Mum began, '…about my daughter's hair.'

The girl looked at the fuzz on top of my head. I wanted to turn and run.

'Yes,' she agreed, as if it was obvious. 'Take a seat and some-one will be straight over.'

I refused to look up because I was convinced everyone was staring at me. Instead I took a seat next to Mum. She flicked through some magazines but I was anxious and started kicking my heels off the wooden bench beside her.

'Stop it!' she snapped.

I glared at the ground. It was her fault I was here. Suddenly, the hairdresser appeared.

'Do you want to come over?' she said, tapping the back of a nearby chair.

The stylist was a heavily-bosomed woman with teased blonde hair, exactly the same shape and colour as a brass bell.

Mum explained the problem and the hairdresser pulled sympathetic faces and tutted as she listened. She ruffled her fingers through the frizz and grimaced at the state of my hair. You could read what she was thinking by the look on her face. But even though she was sympathetic, she refused to do anything with it.

'Her hair's ruined,' she said simply. 'You can either cut it all off and start again or stop using that stuff in it and let it grow out naturally and get its condition back.'

I looked up in horror at Mum through the reflection in the mirror. She was standing behind, nodding her head in agreement.

'I'm not having it cut,' I insisted. 'I'll look like a boy!'

I knew a boy's haircut would make my life a hundred times worse at school.

'Well, in that case you'll just have to grow it out,' the hairdresser told me.

'But how long will that take?' I gasped.

'Months, probably even a year. I'd put a colour over it but I'm afraid the condition is so bad that I'd be too scared to touch it.'

And so my fate was sealed. I was the girl with the golden hair, but I wasn't like the one in the adverts. She was beautiful and successful. I wasn't – I felt stupid and ugly. Instead I became more and more of a sitting target. It took an age but my roots slowly grew out, making the blonde and brown equal in length. I looked ridiculous, as if I really was wearing a wig. All I'd ever wanted to do was blend into the crowd, but my hair wouldn't let me. Instead everyone had a field day at my expense.

The other girls were pretty with nice, shiny hair and they wore the right clothes. I was Mophead, the one everyone laughed at. But fate was about to throw a curveball into my life. Little did I know it then, but I was about to become the envy of every girl in my school.

CHAPTER 5

CARNIVAL QUEEN

E ach year, a carnival procession was held in the centre of town. Made up of dozens of different floats, it was sponsored by local businesses promoting their wares. Everyone looked forward to the gala, especially the kids because it meant the fair would come to town. In many ways, it was the highlight of our summer.

I'd already spent a miserable first year at secondary school. The bullies had made me feel crap about myself every day, so I was looking forward to it, especially the fair with its merry-go-round – it was my favourite ride. Up until now, I'd always been a spectator; I never got involved in the gala because I preferred to just blend into the crowd. Being involved was a job for the popular girls, not me. But Lauren had different ideas.

'Let's dance in the procession, we could join the school dance troupe.' she suggested, her eyes flashing with excitement.

My mouth fell open; I thought she'd gone mad, again. Everyone knew the dance troupe was made up of all the popular girls, not misfits like us. To try and join in would be social suicide.

'Err, no way!' I gasped, but Lauren refused to take no for an answer.

'Come on,' she coaxed. 'We'll be together and it'll be fun!'

But I wasn't having any of it. I thought she'd completely lost her marbles.

'Are you kidding me? They'll slaughter us and you know it. Besides, they all do tap and ballet lessons – they have all the right dance gear, we don't.'

But Lauren shook her head.

'Why shouldn't we?' she said, rising to her feet. 'Don't you think we're good enough, is that it?'

'No, it's not that. You know it's not. It's just…' my voice trailed off. She was right: we *were* better than the rest of them put together when it came to dancing. After all, we practised every night in my bedroom. Maybe it wasn't such a bad idea, after all.

'We know all the Steps dance routines and you're really, really good. This is something we're both good at.' Lauren insisted. 'Remember the school play back in primary?'

She spoke of nothing else until finally I backed down. In the end I agreed to go along to the audition just to shut her up.

'Alright, alright,' I said, holding up my hand in mid-air. 'I'll go. But if they start on me or say *one* thing, I'm out of there.'

Lauren let out an excited squeal and threw her arms around me with excitement.

'We'll be fantastic,' she promised, 'just wait and see!'

On the day of the first rehearsal I felt the panic rise inside me. Primary school was one thing, but secondary school was quite another. If we made a mess of this, our lives wouldn't be worth living.

'I'm not sure this is such a good idea,' I said, changing my mind outside the school hall.

'Come on,' Lauren said, giving me a shove in the back, 'we've come this far, we're going in.'

As soon as they spotted us, the usual whispers started up at the back of the hall.

'What are *they* doing here?' one girl hissed to the others.

'God, all we need is those two!' another said, rolling her eyes.

I gulped. A knot of anxiety twisted in the bottom of my stomach like a blunt knife. My hands and forehead felt clammy with sweat; I knew this wasn't a good idea. I looked at Lauren, but she seemed oblivious. I steeled myself – I owed it to her to give this a try.

Prior to this, and in a bid to get me out of the house and mixing with other children, Mum had enrolled me in a local majorette dance troupe just down the road from where we lived. So, when the teacher showed us the dance routines, I found it easy to keep up. I glanced over at Lauren; she found it easy too. She was right, just as she'd been about the school play: this was something we were good at.

Suddenly I heard a commotion behind me. One of the other girls had gone the wrong way and bumped into a girl next to her, causing her to fall on the floor.

'Watch where you're going, will you!' she hissed.

I looked across at Lauren and winked. We both smirked. It seemed they weren't as good as they thought they were. By the end of the lesson, I was out of breath but I'd really enjoyed myself and I was glad Lauren had suggested it.

Even the teacher commented on how good we were. I felt my chest swell with pride.

'Great, girls, keep working hard like that and I'll have you both up front, showing the rest of them how it's done!'

Lauren grinned with pride. Afterwards we laughed about how rubbish the others were.

'Did you see her?' I giggled, hardly able to control myself. 'She almost went flying when she kicked her leg in the air, the silly cow!'

Lauren held her sides, trying to control her laughter.

'I know – she looked like a baby elephant in that pink leotard!'

It felt good that the popular girls were the butt of the joke for once and not us. And, in a way, it gave us a bit of confidence back. Soon we were rushing to every dance rehearsal in preparation for gala day. The dance troupe had quite literally given me a new lease of life.

'Mum,' I called one night when I got in from school, 'I need to wear a summery outfit with a sarong on the day of the carnival.'

Mum turned to look at me; she'd not seen me this happy in years.

'I can't wait to see you and Lauren,' she said, 'I bet you two are really good, aren't you?'

'Well, we're not bad,' I grinned. 'The teacher says she might even put us up front if we practise hard.'

'Wow!' said Mum, raising her eyebrows. 'I'll pop into town first thing tomorrow morning and I'll buy you the brightest and prettiest sarong in the shop!'

As carnival day drew closer, my nerves set in. What if I messed up the dance routine? What if I tripped and fell over? My mind was plagued with all the things that could go wrong.

The bullying had subsided a little since we'd started in the dance troupe and I didn't want it starting up again. If I made a mess of the routine, they'd be sure to use it against me. Soon, I was worrying so much that I found it hard to sleep. Part of me wanted carnival day to arrive but the other half wanted it to be all over and done with.

On the day, I climbed out of bed and pulled open my bedroom curtains. It was sunny and warm, a beautiful day for the procession. I told myself it was a sign everything would be okay. I pulled my dressing gown around me, tied the belt and headed down for breakfast. Mum was already downstairs in the kitchen when I walked through the door.

'Cereal?' she asked, shaking the packet at me.

'Uh-huh,' I muttered, before stretching and yawning. Exhausted, I flopped down into a chair at the table.

'Well, I hope you're going to liven up before the carnival. Me and your dad are coming to watch you and we don't want to see you asleep in front of one of those floats!' she teased, putting the bowl down in front of me.

I grinned, poured some ice-cold milk over my breakfast and tucked in.

Half an hour later I was up in my bedroom, tying the sarong around my waist, when I heard the back door open. A woman's voice spoke downstairs and I recognised it immediately – it was my aunt Sarah.

'Is Katie in?' she asked, loud and urgent.

'Yeah,' Mum replied, 'she's just getting…'

But before she had a chance to finish Aunt Sarah was climbing the stairs.

'Katie, Katie!' she gasped, 'I need to speak to you.'

I ran out onto the landing to see my aunt being closely

followed by Mum. But Mum looked as puzzled as I did. My aunt sounded really excited about something.

'Katie,' Aunt Sarah said, 'How do you fancy being the Carnival Queen?'

My mouth fell open. I looked from my aunt to Mum and back again, then shook my head in disbelief.

'*Me*?' I asked, as though she'd made a mistake.

Aunt Sarah nodded and clasped her hands together. 'I know,' she squealed, 'it's fantastic, isn't it?'

Mum covered her mouth in shock. For a split second she didn't know what to say but she soon found her voice.

'Hang on, I thought they already had a carnival queen?'

'They did,' my aunt replied, 'but she's sick so we have a dress, a crown and a float but no Queen. They didn't know what to do so I've suggested Katie!'

It transpired that my aunt was best friends with the organiser, a lady called Debbie. So, when they needed a little girl at short notice, she'd put my name forward.

Mum's face beamed with excitement. 'Of course she'll do it, won't you, Katie?'

Both women turned to face me. I was stunned and excited at the same time but I was also apprehensive. I pulled at the sarong around my waist – I was scared. What would the bullies say? Wouldn't it just make things ten times worse if I was Queen for the day? I'd be the most important person in the parade and they'd all have something to say about that.

'I'm not sure,' I began, my voice edged with nerves, 'it's just…well, I'm already in the dance group and the others…I don't know what they'd say…and…'

Aunt Sarah's face fell, but Mum was having none of it.

'Of course you'll do it, Katie – it's a once-in-a-lifetime

opportunity. Anyway, you'll make a beautiful Queen,' she said, smoothing my hair with the palm of her hand.

Her words stuck inside my head. A beautiful Queen – I could be Queen for the day. Mum was right; this was my chance to prove to all those girls at school that I wasn't ugly and useless: I was clever and pretty enough to be Queen. This would show them once and for all.

'Okay,' I said, biting my lip, 'as long as you're sure I'll be okay?'

My aunt grabbed me by the shoulders.

'You'll be brilliant, Katie!' she squealed. 'You'll make a fantastic Gala Queen!'

'Right,' she said, fumbling for her mobile phone, 'I'll call Debbie and tell her the good news.'

Within the hour, my trademark half-blonde, half-brown hair had been backcombed and teased to within an inch of its life and scraped into a bun. After spraying a tonne of hairspray on me, Debbie gently placed the Carnival Queen crown on my head.

'Beautiful!' she said, looking back at Mum and Aunt Sarah, who both nodded in agreement.

I tip-toed into my dress. It had been loaned by a local wedding dress shop for the day and it was gorgeous.

'Careful,' said Mum, as I pulled up the ivory ball gown. I considered myself in the bedroom mirror and gasped; I looked and felt lovely. For the first time in my life I was truly beautiful.

'Turn round so we can all see,' Mum urged.

I twirled and my aunt, Debbie and Mum all sighed collectively.

'Pretty as a picture,' Aunt Sarah gasped. I looked up at her gratefully.

'You look beautiful, Katie,' Mum sighed. 'Really beautiful.'

'Steve,' Mum shouted downstairs to Dad, 'come up here and look at your beautiful daughter!'

Dad's eyes filled with pride as soon as he saw me.

'You look gorgeous, darling,' he said, holding out his hands. I ran over to him and he scooped me up in his big, strong arms.

'Thanks, Dad,' I said, tears in my eyes. But they were happy tears – I couldn't believe this was really happening.

We were running late and there was no time to waste. My hair and make-up had taken an age to do and I'd been powdered and preened to perfection.

Dad ran downstairs to the drive and started up the car engine. He shouted at us to hurry up.

'Come on,' he said as he tooted the car horn, 'we can't keep them waiting!'

As we sped along the country lanes, I gripped the posy of flowers tight in my hand and glanced out of the car window. It had all happened so fast – my head was whirring. I was going to be Queen for the day. I couldn't wait until the nasty girls saw me; they'd be pea-green with envy.

Ten minutes later, Dad parked the car and Mum helped me out of the back seat. It was a beautiful dress but it wasn't very easy to walk in. The sun was high up in the sky. I raised a gloved hand against my eyes to shield them, frightened the heat would cause my make-up to run. I was still looking at the gathering crowds when I spotted Lauren in the distance. She was alone, waiting for me. My heart sank when I noticed she was dressed in her dance outfit. I felt guilty; I should've been with her but now she'd have to go it alone. I shouted and waved, and Lauren turned. As soon as she saw me her face changed. She looked confused when she saw the ivory ball gown. I beckoned her over and she came running towards me.

'What are you dressed like that for? Where's your sarong?' she gasped, a little out of breath. 'I thought you weren't coming.' she added but she couldn't stop looking at my outfit.

'Katie,' she asked, 'why are you dressed like that?'

I took a deep breath.

'They've asked me to be Carnival Queen for the day. My aunt came to the house this morning; the real Queen was sick. They needed a replacement so they asked me.'

The words came out quick and garbled.

Lauren's face changed as the penny dropped.

'You mean *you're* the Carnival Queen?' she gasped, her jaw falling open with shock.

'Yep,' I said, giving her a twirl. Suddenly doubt gripped me.

'Lauren, do I…do I look okay?' I asked.

But Lauren was shaking her head as if she still couldn't believe it.

'Katie,' she said, taking a step back, 'you look amazing, honestly, you do.'

A warm feeling flooded my body. This would be alright. I was so caught up in the excitement that at first, I didn't notice Lauren's face clouded with sadness.

'Oh Lauren, I'm sorry. Are you going to be okay, on your own?'

But she didn't speak, instead she just shrugged.

'I'd rather have you with me, but don't worry, I'll be fine. Besides, I know the routine off by heart.'

Suddenly, a mischievous look washed over her face.

'I'll tell you what, though. I can't wait to see their faces when they see you dressed as the Queen!'

'I know!' I squealed. With that we both dissolved into a fit of giggles.

Suddenly, Aunt Sarah stepped forward.

'Katie, there you are! I've been looking for you everywhere. It's time to go.'

'See you later then,' I said, grabbing Lauren's hand one last time for luck.

'See you,' she replied. 'And Katie,' she said, turning back to face me, 'good luck!'

Moments later, a man I didn't know lifted me up into a plastic chair. It was swathed in a white sheet and surrounded with tubs full of pink, red and orange pansy flowers. A little girl and boy were already on the float, sitting either side of my 'throne'.

'We're your attendants,' the little girl whispered, taking my hand. She was as nervous as I was.

'It's okay,' I soothed. 'I'll look after you.'

The little girl smiled up at me and, for the first time in ages, I felt special.

With a sudden jolt, the engine started up and the float lunged forward – we were off on our way. As we turned the corner towards the start point, I felt the familiar knot of anxiety twist in the pit of my stomach. Thankfully, we weren't at the front of the parade but in the middle – like the jewel in the crown. In some ways it made it worse. What if people were disappointed when they saw Katie Taylor sitting on the throne?

My body jangled with fear and I found myself crippled with self-doubt. *What was I doing? Who did I think I was? What if they laughed at me?*

These thoughts raced through my mind as the music started up and the parade began. I gasped when I saw the crowd, and what seemed to be hundreds of people lining the street.

Parents and children glanced up from the path below. Little

ones pointed up at me. Their mouths were wide-open in awe, as if they were seeing a real-life princess.

Suddenly a lone voice carried high above the music and the sound of the crowd.

'Oh my God, it's Katie Taylor!' the voice called; it was loud and it rose above the other noise.

I turned to see the ugly freckle-faced boy from my class. He was laughing and nudging his mates. In a flash, I was back in the classroom. The bullies were there, watching, laughing and pointing at me. But this was worse: now I was high up on a throne where everyone could see me – there was nowhere to hide. Despite the heavy pan stick make-up I felt myself flush. They'd tear me apart.

Oh God, here we go… I thought.

I took a deep breath. My nerves were getting the better of me as my stomach churned like a washing machine. I felt sick but the float was moving and there was no escape.

I'll just have to grit my teeth and get through this, I told myself. I wanted the ground to swallow me up as the boy shouted louder so that everyone could hear.

'Look, it's Katie Taylor – the ugliest Carnival Queen you've ever seen!' he hollered. He was laughing, but then I realised no one else was: he was on his own. I felt a glimmer of hope.

The boy continued to jeer and call out but I ignored him and stared straight ahead. I had to do this, and I would. I'd do it for Debbie, Aunt Sarah, Mum and Dad, but most of all, I'd do it for myself.

Just then I spotted a few familiar faces craning their necks from the front of the parade. It was the girls from the dance troupe and they were trying to get a better look. Now they knew it was me who was the Carnival Queen, I wondered

what they'd say. I thought of poor Lauren up there with them.
I had to do this for her as well, to show them that they weren't
better than us.

Nervously, I held out my hand and began to wave. As I
did so, I heard the crowd clap and cheer. People waved back
at me and everyone was smiling. It spurred me on. A rush of
joy flooded through me. I could do this, and I would. I waved
my hand again and a small child waved back as if I was the
Queen herself. The more I waved, the more applause I got.
For the first time in my life I felt special – it felt good. Soon
I was waving and smiling at everyone we passed, even the
nasty kids from school. The shock on their faces when they
saw I was Queen made me laugh even more. It had been
worthwhile, all the worry and stress – it was priceless. Slowly
the parade wound down the main street. I smiled serenely
as if I was truly meant to be there. No one could touch
me now.

Eventually, we came to a stop at the funfair and my day as
Queen was over. Mum and Dad were standing alongside my
brother Andrew. My parents' faces were full of pride.

'Here she is,' Dad cheered, his arms outstretched, 'here's my
little princess!'

Mum grabbed the camera and Andrew rolled his eyes. He
didn't like me being the centre of attention, but I loved it!

'Katie, let me get a photo quick,' Mum said, as she began to
snap away.

Out of the corner of my eye I spotted the dance troupe
crowding round to get a better look. Their faces contorted with
jealousy – angry arms folded across their flat chests. They were
whispering too, but I knew they wouldn't say anything, not
with Mum and Dad there.

Mum took dozens more pictures and eventually Aunt Sarah came dashing over.

'Well done, Katie, you looked amazing!' she gasped, planting a kiss on top of my head.

'Thanks,' I replied. I *felt* amazing.

'When she's ready, bring the dress over to me and I'll pop it back in the bag,' she told Mum. But I never wanted to take the dress off because then the magic would be gone. I wanted to wear it forever. Then my life would always feel this good. I felt amazing, if only for a day, and I wanted to stay that way forever. But soon it was time to change back into my old clothes and my old life.

'Here,' said Dad, noticing my disappointment, 'here's some money. Go and spend it on the merry-go-round.'

He dropped several pound coins into my hand so I dashed over to my favourite ride. I chose the biggest and prettiest horse I could see – a beautiful white stallion with a blue saddle and sky-blue eyes. As I bobbed up and down, I imagined galloping as far as I could from the town and the bullies. The ride spun faster and the fairground whizzed by in a blur. I closed my eyes. This was the happiest day of my life and I didn't want it to end. Dad wrapped an arm around Mum's waist and the sun was hot in the sky; everything was perfect. I'd been Queen for the day and everyone had seen.

I was tired but happy as I climbed into my bed later that night. But a niggling doubt wouldn't go away; it gnawed its way through the back of my mind. I wasn't really a Queen; I was just plain old Katie Taylor and I always would be.

I knew what the others thought and now I was certain they'd make my life a misery. They'd make me pay for today. I'd pay for that one tiny slice of happiness.

CHAPTER 6

THE NEW GIRL

'How come you got chosen for Carnival Queen?' Melanie, the nasty blonde girl sneered. She trapped me with her arms against the classroom wall. Her piggy blue eyes narrowed when she spoke.

There were other girls there too. They were egging her on. Melanie put her hand on her hip and waited for my answer but I didn't know what to say. It infuriated her even more.

'You're too ugly to be Carnival Queen,' she yelled, 'Everyone knows it! Why would they pick you, Katie Taylor? They should have picked one of us,' she said, looking back at the rest of the group, who nodded in unison.

Fear caught at the back of my throat. But she wasn't finished.

'I should have been Carnival Queen, not you, because I'm loads prettier.'

I stared blankly at her face. She wasn't pretty at all. Her face was contorted and twisted with jealousy. In that moment, I realised just how ugly she really was. But my silence wound her up even more. Holding out the palm of her hand, she gave me a hard shove in the chest. I fell backwards, trapping my school rucksack behind me. My pencil case dug in as Melanie pinned me there and stuck her face in front of mine. She was so close that I could see the spit on her teeth. She looked vicious and wild, like an animal.

More children gathered round and circled us, thinking a fight was about to break out.

'You're too ugly and thick to be Carnival Queen,' Melanie sneered, her spit showering my face. It felt disgusting. She glanced back at her audience and then at me. My whole body trembled with fear.

'Can you imagine Mophead as the Gala Queen?' she laughed. 'Now that's the biggest joke of all 'cos she's the ugliest girl in school!'

The others laughed. Suddenly a rage welled up inside me. The words came spilling out before I had the chance to stop them.

'Yes,' I snapped, pushing her away. I stood up straight and looked her square in the eye. 'But you can't be *that* pretty, Melanie, otherwise it *would* have been you up there on that throne, and not me!'

The room fell silent. Katie Taylor, the girl who had no voice, had suddenly found one. No one knew what to say. Suddenly, Melanie's eyes narrowed as she tried to think of something to say but nothing would come. I'd just taken the wind out of her sails. It was the first time I'd really stood up for myself and it felt good. *Really* good. I realised that I'd won, this time.

Finally, one of the other girls tapped her on the shoulder. 'Leave her, Mel,' she mumbled. 'She's not worth it.'

Melanie stopped to consider me for a second longer, her eyes full of hatred.

'Yes,' she agreed, 'you're right, she's not worth it and she never will be. You'll always be a loser,' she hissed at me.

Then she turned and walked away; the rest of the group followed. I wondered how someone so horrid could hold so much power. I looked at the others still but no one would look at me. I was surrounded by people but I'd never felt so alone. Pulling up a sleeve, I glanced at my watch – it was still early. I prayed for the time to pass and for Megan to arrive soon.

The girls were still whispering about me at the back of the classroom when the first lesson began. Some were intrigued and a few even approached me to ask questions in first break.

How come you were chosen? How did you get to be the Gala Queen? They all wanted to know. Of course, I didn't tell them the real reason. Instead I simply shrugged my shoulders.

'I was just asked, that's all,' I replied.

Occasionally throughout the day, I caught them looking. I could tell what they were thinking. *Why, in a town full of pretty girls, was Katie Taylor chosen?*

They didn't say it but they didn't have to; it was written all over their faces. The question was burning inside them. Of course I never told them the real reason that I'd only ended up in the role by default. I wanted them to believe I'd been chosen because I was pretty. I wanted them to stand in my shoes for a change.

But as the days passed, the name calling got worse. Melanie wouldn't let it go and by now she'd assembled a whole army behind her, including the boys. It was as if nothing had changed. My Carnival Queen moment had passed and now it was back to reality with a bump.

When the boys said I was too ugly to be Carnival Queen, I thought my heart would break. I'd had a secret crush on a few of them but now I felt ugly. I convinced myself I was ugly – I'd never get a boyfriend now. No one would ever want to go out with me.

Later that day, I trudged in from school as if I carried the weight of the world on my shoulders. I threw my school bag down on the floor and hung my coat up on the usual peg but as I did so, all the hurt and emotion I'd been holding inside bubbled up to the surface. Tears welled until my eyes were full and everything came spilling out. Mum heard me cry and came running over.

'Katie,' she said, taking me in her arms, 'whatever's the matter?'

The look on her face made me sob even more. I never told her how hard my life at school was– she had no idea, neither did Dad. They knew nothing about the bullying I faced every day. I was beginning to wish I'd never agreed to be the stupid Queen.

As the words came tumbling out Mum said nothing, she just listened.

'They call me ugly,' I wept. 'They say I'm too ugly to be Gala Queen. Maybe they're right?'

But Mum was having none of it. She grabbed my face and held it tight in her hands to get my full attention.

'Now listen here, Katie Taylor. You were chosen because you are pretty, do you hear me?'

Her voice rose as if she was angry, but I knew she wasn't angry with me.

'You are lovely, Katie – never forget that. You are worth a million of them. Do you hear me?' Mum said, clasping my face in her hands.

'Okay,' I whispered and nodded forlornly.

But it was alright for Mum; she didn't have to go to school every day and listen to the nasty comments. I did, but that was my life and I'd just have to get used to it.

Soon Megan, Lauren and I became friends with another girl called Beth. She sat next to me in most of my lessons. Like us, Beth wasn't part of the popular gang, so we let her join ours. Together, we promised to look out for one another.

A few days later, we were in a PE lesson when the teacher explained we'd be doing fitness tests. The aim of the lesson was to run between two points. A bleep would sound and you had to reach the other side of the room before it bleeped again. I tried my best to run to the other side of the hall but it was hopeless, I just wasn't as fast as the others.

'Look, the Carnival Queen isn't very clever now, is she?' Melanie taunted from the back of the hall. I stared at her.

Soon the bleeps got even closer together and try as I might, I just wasn't quick enough.

'God, you're so unfit,' another girl sneered. The others heard her and giggled. Shame-faced, I hung my head as I walked to the end of the line.

I didn't know why I wasn't as good as the others. Maybe it was because I had started to believe them when they told me how useless I was? The only thing I was certain of was that my confidence was draining out of me daily, like grains of sand in an hourglass.

'Just ignore them,' Lauren said later in the cloakroom, when I told her about it. 'They'll soon get bored and move onto the next thing.'

I wanted to believe her but it was hard to think this would ever come to an end. However, after a month, Lauren's words came true.

STOLEN GIRL

A new girl arrived in school one Monday morning. Her name was Donna. She was an odd-looking girl with dark frizzy hair and glasses. She didn't look girly like the others, instead she was quirky and individual, just like us. We soon discovered that she'd left another school in the area to move to ours but we didn't know why.

At first, the popular girls were all over her like a rash. They wanted to know why she'd moved to our school and left her old one half-way through term. They wanted to know her secrets so that they could use them against her. It took all the strength I had not to wade into the middle of the group just to warn her but it was no good, I couldn't get close. Even from where I was sitting, I could see Donna was nothing like them. I knew that before long, they'd chew her up and spit her out, just like they did everyone else.

I watched as she shifted uneasily in her seat when they fired question after question at her. She squirmed under the intense spotlight. Like us, she didn't fit in and she knew it. Whilst part of me felt sorry for her, another part wanted to give her a wide berth – life was difficult enough without someone else to look out for.

Once lessons began it was apparent why Donna had left her last school: she struggled with the simplest of tasks. I watched in English as she traced a finger along the page of the book, mouthing each word silently to herself as she read. She read her book like a five-year-old. I thought it odd. The book wasn't even difficult yet she seemed to struggle and she never put her hand up in class. She wasn't much better at maths either. Soon, I wasn't the dumbest girl in the class anymore – poor Donna was given the title. Almost immediately, the popular girls drifted away from her. Her newness wore off and now no one wanted to know. I felt a pang of guilt when I saw her on her own at break times, sad, lonely and left out. I knew I ought to help but something told me to stay away – I had enough to deal with without asking for more trouble.

So a few days later, when one of the popular girls approached and started being over-friendly, I was naturally suspicious. As always, there was a reason behind it.

'Listen, we're supposed to be looking after Donna but could you do it instead?' she said.

I looked at Lauren and Beth.

'Why?' I asked. I didn't want Donna in our group, she was odd and things were hard enough without having to look after her.

'It's just that we think she'll fit in more with your group than ours,' the girl said. She preened her hair as she spoke. I wanted to slap her.

I turned and looked back at the others in horror. She was basically saying that because Donna was an oddball, she'd blend in with our group. I felt utterly insulted but I also realised then that Donna had no one else; we had to help.

Donna wasn't thick, she just couldn't read or write. It wasn't her fault, she had dyslexia. That's why she'd left her last school, because her life had been made a misery with constant bullying. When I heard, I wanted to help because I knew what it felt like when people labelled you 'thick'.

'People think I'm stupid but there's something wrong with my eyes,' she explained. 'When I try to read the words just jump and move about on the page. I try to trace them with my finger but nothing works, nothing keeps them still. I can't do anything about it. I try my best but it's like they're always jiggling and dancing around.'

Lauren and I looked at one another in astonishment.

'What, you mean you can't read anything?' Megan asked bluntly.

Donna shook her head sadly. I decided then that not only would we protect her, but I'd try my best to help her too. English was something I was good at. If anyone could help, it was me. But by befriending her, our group had taken on a whole new heap of trouble.

'Watch out, here comes Mophead and her freaks,' a boy hissed as we passed by.

I turned to the others. I didn't say a word because I didn't have to, we all knew what we had to do. Within seconds we'd surrounded him. There were five of us now. Our ranks were swelling – there was safety in numbers and now we could defend ourselves.

The boy smirked nervously as we crowded around him.

'Yeah, you and whose army?' he sneered, but then he saw the look on our faces and knew we weren't joking anymore. There was one of him, but five of us.

'Only kidding, girls,' he shrugged, holding his hands out.

'Come on,' I said, shooting him one last filthy look. With that we turned and walked away.

With Lauren in a different class, Beth and I became inseparable. We'd sit next to each other in lessons and hang around at lunch times together. When we walked along the corridor, we'd often link arms. Other girls did the same too and no one said a word, but when we did it the others called us gay.

'Watch out, here come the lesbians!' they would chant whenever we approached. I didn't care because I was becoming more confident. Finally, I was toughening up and sometimes I even stood up to them; it felt good. There were five of us now, we were a unit and together we could look after ourselves.

Only Donna wasn't as strong as we thought she was. The constant bullying, even in the safety of a group, eventually ground her down. She'd had enough and, after only a few months, she left without a word. I arrived one morning to find her desk and chair empty. It felt symbolic somehow; maybe we weren't as strong as I thought we were.

'Where's Donna, Miss?' I asked the teacher.

'She's gone,' she replied, without even looking up. She flicked through a pile of books on top of her desk.

'Gone where?' I asked.

'She's gone, left the school,' she snapped. 'Now please leave me alone, Katie, I have books to mark.'

Our friend had simply vanished without a word. She didn't even stop to say goodbye, she just left. I felt sad, disappointed she hadn't been stronger. It was as if she'd simply given up – and I felt that by leaving she'd let both us and herself down. I wondered how many other schools she'd have to go through before she stopped running. Would she ever stop running away from herself and her problems?

I felt slightly envious of Donna because there had been many a time when I'd wished I could have run away, but I soon learnt life isn't like that. If you have problems, they don't simply vanish just because you choose to. Wherever you go, your problems go too. They have a habit of packing themselves up and following you around like a shadow.

I still felt sad when I arrived home from school. Mum wasn't in the kitchen as usual. I thought it odd – she always cooked us a hot meal before leaving for work. But tonight the kitchen was cold. Suddenly, I heard raised voices up above me. It was Mum and Dad – they were arguing in the bedroom. Their voices were loud but muffled and distorted by the closed door. I tried to listen but couldn't quite work out what they were saying. The argument brewed into something else and from that day on it spread like a virus through our home and throughout their marriage. After that, they seemed to argue the whole time as if they'd lost all the love they'd once held for one another.

The timing was strange because despite Donna suddenly leaving school, for the first time in years, my life had become more settled. I no longer lived in constant fear because now I had my own gang and I felt as if, for once, I truly belonged. But just as I'd begun to feel more content at school, so my home life took a turn for the worse.

CHAPTER 7

THE DAY MY LIFE CHANGED

The atmosphere at home was now so awful that I'd dawdle all the way home from school. Mum and Dad were arguing more and more, and the house was always full of shouting. Accusations were thrown like poison arrows across the kitchen table. I didn't know what was going on and part of me didn't want to because, whatever it was, I knew it was something bad. I'd never ever seen them argue like this before.

It's hard being a child when your parents fall out of love with one another. Part of the situation makes you believe that somewhere, amongst all the rows and petty misgivings, they love you just that little bit less. I hated the shouting and every time they argued I wanted to stand on my chair and scream until they stopped. Deep down I knew it wouldn't make any difference; even if I did scream, I wondered if they'd even notice. In the end, I decided not to get caught up in it all. I reckoned the more I dragged my feet on the way home, the less I'd have to listen to.

One day, when I pushed open the front door, I realised there were no raised voices. Instead, the house was silent. In fact, it was so quiet the silence was deafening.

I sniffed at the air. There was no smell of cooking either. Instead the house smelled of dust, as though it was dead.

'Mum?' I called, but there was no reply.

I heard someone shush their voice. The noise was slight, barely a whisper but I followed it all the way to the kitchen. The door was closed, which was unusual. It was always open, but not tonight.

She must be in there, I told myself. *Maybe she was hiding? Maybe she was behind the door, waiting to pounce out and shout 'boo!'...*

I burst in through the kitchen door with a huge grin on my face; this had to be a wind-up. But when I opened it, Mum wasn't there, only Dad. He was sitting at the kitchen table, his head in his hands, and he looked exhausted. My eyes shifted to someone else standing beside him. A tall, slim dark-haired man I'd never seen before. It was odd because neither man was speaking; Dad stared straight ahead whilst the strange man looked anxiously over at me. A forced silence hung in the air but it felt like it was packed with explosives, as though something might go off at any moment. I looked at Dad and then at the man but no one said a word. I knew I'd interrupted an important conversation, one I wasn't privy to. Then it dawned on me: they'd shut up the moment I'd come through the front door, that's what the 'Shush!' had been. Dad had a secret he didn't want me to know, but who was the man? I was only twelve, but I was old enough to sense the atmosphere between them. Something wasn't right.

My father's face looked tired and drawn as if he'd not slept a wink. The strange man seemed jittery and nervous as if he wasn't sure whether or not he should say hello.

'Where's Mum?' I demanded.

Both Dad and the strange man flinched at the mention of her name. I didn't know the man and I was sure that Mum wouldn't know him either, so why was he looking at me like that?

Dad's eyes were sad and somehow he suddenly looked older.

'She's at Diane's,' he said, pointing his hand in the direction of our neighbour's house.

Diane was the same age as Mum and lived a few doors away from us at the bottom of the road. They were good friends and were always popping into each other's houses for a cup of tea. It wasn't odd that Mum was there but it was strange that she wasn't here making tea and getting ready to leave for work. I closed the front door and ran to Diane's house to find out what was going on.

My heart beat fast as everything raced through my mind. I thought about the cold cooker, no tea, the strange man standing in our kitchen…Who was he? Dad hadn't even introduced him, yet usually that's the first thing he would've done because that's how my dad is – friendly and polite. Nothing made much sense.

Grabbing the gate to Diane's front garden, I pulled it up high on its hinges so it would open. The gate had been like that for as long as I could remember. Diane had nagged her husband Chris to fix it time and time again but he was always busy with something else – fixing his car mostly, she complained.

I walked around the side of the house towards the back door. Diane had known me since I was a baby; she would have been shocked if I'd have knocked at the front. Clenching my fist, I tapped lightly on the glass. I didn't even wait for an answer – it wasn't how you did things around there. Diane's door was always open to us.

'Mum?' I called out before the door had even fully opened.

I stumbled into Diane's kitchen to find them both sitting at the table. Diane looked a little startled when she saw me – as surprised as the strange man had been. A pot of tea sat sadly in the middle of the kitchen table. There were two mugs in front of them. They were full to the brim with strong builder's tea but they looked untouched, stagnant and stone cold. I guessed just by looking at them that Mum must have been there for ages.

As soon as she saw me, Diane became anxious. Her eyes darted nervously between me and Mum, who still had her back to me. Something was up. I noticed Diane wringing her hands in her lap, as if she wasn't quite sure what to say. The atmosphere in the kitchen was the same as it had been at home.

'Mum,' I said again, my voice a little weaker. 'There's a strange man in our house, talking to Dad.'

Mum didn't respond or turn around but remained seated. She was slim and I could see the outline of her spine – her shoulders hunched over down towards the table as though she'd given up. Even though I couldn't see her face, I knew she was upset about something.

'Is everything alright?' I asked, even though I really didn't want to know the answer.

Diane subconsciously twisted her wedding ring nervously around her finger as Mum turned to face me. Her eyes looked red, as if she'd been crying all afternoon. As she moved, I spotted something behind her – a bunch of screwed-up tissues. They were scattered all over the table. A sob caught in the back of my throat. Something was wrong and whatever it was, it was serious because Mum never cried. Never. Yet here she was, crying in Diane's kitchen. I tried not to let my fear show; whatever it was, I wanted her to think I was grown up enough to handle it. But I needed to know what was going on and who the strange man was.

Mum's voice cracked with emotion as she spoke.

'Everything's fine, Katie – just go back home, will you? I'll be there soon.'

But I didn't want to go back home – I wanted to be with Mum. I wanted to know why she was crying in Diane's house and who the strange man was making Dad look so sad back home. But Mum refused to tell me any more.

'Katie, go home. Please,' she said, her eyes as tired as my father's.

I felt stuck. I didn't want to go back to the house with the strange man in it; I didn't want to leave Mum crying and upset. I didn't know what to do for the best. Diane came over. She wrapped her arm around my shoulders and tried her best to reassure me.

'Don't worry, Katie – your mum's just a little bit upset. Be a good girl now and go home. Don't worry, I'll look after her here – she'll be fine here with me.'

With that she opened up the back door and guided me out through it. I felt a slight push in the small of my back as the door closed abruptly behind me. It was a rude thing to do but as I stood alone on Diane's driveway, I knew something bad had happened and guessed it was to do with the strange man.

Tugging at my school socks, I hoisted them back up and ran out through the gate to our house. I'd confront them both, I decided. I'd make Dad tell me who the strange man was. But by the time I arrived, the man had gone.

'Who was he?' I asked.

Dad shifted uneasily in his seat. He was still sitting at the kitchen table. Like Mum, he was hunched over as if he was hugging the table – as though he'd had the stuffing knocked clean out of him.

'No one, Katie. He was no one,' Dad insisted. He pulled himself up and dragged his feet over to the kitchen door, walking like an old man. As he did so, he turned to face me.

'Fix yourself a snack for tea, Katie. Mum will be back soon.'

But I knew he was lying. I could tell Mum wasn't coming home soon; her tears had given her away. I wasn't hungry either – I felt sick. I wanted to be there in Diane's kitchen, where the grown-ups were talking. I wanted to know why my mum was red-eyed from crying and why the strange man had come to our house and left Dad looking so devastated. But they wouldn't tell me.

Life carried on as before but strangely without the constant arguments. Instead, Mum and Dad moved around the house as though they were robots. They said 'please' and 'thank you', but I noticed something else: Dad didn't put his arms around Mum's waist the way he used to. There were no more smiles or jollities. He'd stopped slapping her on the bum when she washed up at the kitchen sink, too. It was as though something had shifted overnight.

We survived like this for the next month or so. My parents still went for the odd night out but they never went together anymore. Mum would go out with friends to the pub or she'd pop in to see them on the way home from work, but she never went out with Dad. When she was at home, she always looked so distracted. Before, she'd notice everything but not anymore. Now it was as if she was just going through the motions of family life, playing her 'role' of mother and wife but her heart wasn't in it, it was obvious. Whenever she cooked it was as if she was standing in our kitchen but her mind was a thousand miles away.

One day as I approached home on my way back from school, I could hear shouting. I was startled when I spotted Mum and Dad standing in the front of their bedroom window – it was wide open and they were screaming at one another. Dad's voice was so loud it carried down the street – everyone could hear him. I cringed when I noticed a few of our neighbours had already come outside to get a better look.

Mum and Dad were struggling with something. Mum was trying to pull something out of Dad's hands but I couldn't make out what it was. She was pleading with him as if she was pleading for her life.

'Don't, Steve. Please…' she begged. Her voice was pitiful.

Something flashed as it fell out of the open window. I held my breath. For a moment, I thought one of them had slipped and fallen but then it landed with a flutter and I realised it was a bundle of clothes – Mum's clothes. I gasped. Mum's best dresses were tangled together in a mess; one even looked as if it'd been torn at the side. More followed. Soon dresses, shirts, trousers, even her underwear was billowing around on the front lawn.

Oh my God, I thought, *Dad has gone mad!*

A few of the local kids pulled up on their bikes to get a better look. They started pointing and laughing at something and then I saw it – a pair of mum's knickers caught in a bush underneath the front window.

Thud!

More stuff fell to the ground: make-up, a hairdryer, even a few of Mum's ornaments, which she kept on the bedside table.

Then I noticed Dad hanging out of the bedroom window, throwing Mum's stuff out as wide into the air as he could. His eyes were wild with fury.

'Please, Steve…the neighbours!' Mum screamed.

My heart lurched. I wanted to die right there and then. More front doors opened and now people were standing in their gardens watching the show – the one featuring Dad having some kind of meltdown. I was terrified. I'd never seen him this angry before. Normally when he lost his temper Mum would calm him down, but not now – he wasn't listening. Then it struck me: maybe he'd listen to me?

I ran in through the front door and bounded up the stairs, two at a time, until I reached the landing. Dad was still manically pulling things off hangers inside the wardrobe. The wooden drawers had already been yanked opened and cleaned out. He'd emptied each and every one of them.

'Not that – please! Steve, please, think of the kids…' Mum pleaded.

'I don't care,' Dad was shouting. 'You've made your bed and now you'll have to lie in it.'

'Dad!' I screamed from the bedroom doorway. 'Please stop!'

The sound of my voice made my father freeze to the spot. He turned to look at me, his eyes wild with anger. But it wasn't aimed at me, this was about Mum – this was something she'd done.

'It's not me, Katie, it's your mother. Ask her, go on, ask her what she's been doing!' Dad shouted, pointing over at Mum. His voice was hoarse, bitter and angry – something he never was. He spat the words out as if they were venom in his mouth. It frightened me because I'd never heard him sound like this before.

Tears brimmed in my eyes; they were tearing each other apart. Whatever it was, it was something really bad.

'Mum?' I asked, hoping for an explanation, but she wouldn't look at me. Dad saw and threw her stuff on the floor.

'I'll tell her, shall I?' he hissed. 'Tell her what you've been up to?'

What was he talking about? My heart quickened with fear.

'It's your mother, Katie,' Dad screamed. 'She's got a boyfriend!'

My mouth fell open, it couldn't be true. Boyfriend? But Mum was married to Dad. I looked at her, but her head was down and her eyes refused to meet mine. Then I waited. I waited for her to deny it, to say that Dad had got it wrong but instead there was a horrible silence.

'Mum?' I whimpered. But she wouldn't look at me, never mind answer. In the end Dad broke the silence.

'She won't tell you, Katie. See, you and Andrew think she's so perfect, but she isn't. All this time she's been carrying on with some fella,' said Dad, spitting out the words.

'Who?' I demanded; now hot and angry tears were flowing down my cheeks. 'Who is it?'

'Remember the man in the kitchen?' Dad sneered, grabbing the last of Mum's clothes off the floor. He bunched them up in his hands. 'Well, she's been seeing him. Yes, that's right – your wonderful mother has been sleeping with someone else.'

I shook my head in disbelief and begged Mum to tell me he was wrong, that he was lying. But she didn't. The look on her face gave her away; Dad's anger gave her away. My father never lied, but it seemed that my mother had. She'd lied to him and us. I thought back to Mum, the day I found her crying in Diane's kitchen – now everything made sense.

'Mum,' I sobbed, my bottom lip beginning to quiver. 'Mum, you're not leaving us, are you?' I gasped. The words were so painful that they caught in my throat as if edged with broken glass.

But Mum wouldn't answer. Instead, she barged past us into the hallway and fled downstairs. I heard her pick up the telephone and dial a number. Dad heard her too – it seemed to make him even worse.

'And she can take these things with her,' he said, hurling the rest of her clothes out through the open window.

Mum was talking to someone on the phone but she wasn't talking in a normal voice – instead she was shouting loud enough so Dad could hear. They were both acting like children, as though this was a game and they were point-scoring to see who could hurt who the most.

'Yes, he's throwing my clothes out the bedroom window right now,' she said, as if giving a running commentary, 'Yes, the whole street's watching us. He knows everything and so do the kids.'

Then I realised who it was – it was *him*. Mum was talking to the strange man on our home telephone. At that moment she laughed – it was enough to tip me over the edge. I stood shaking with anger at the top of the stairs and saw red as I watched Mum laughing and flirting with someone I didn't even know. She was talking to the strange man, the stranger who'd ruined everything, the stranger who was taking my mum away from me.

I raced down the stairs and snatched the phone out of her hand.

'I hate you!' I screamed down the phone. 'You're a fucking bastard!' A wild fury rose up inside me as the words streamed out of my mouth. I didn't care that I was swearing in front of Mum and Dad, or at the strange man at the other end of the line.

'You're not taking my mum away from me, understand?' I screamed.

Mum snatched the phone from my hand and turned away. I felt utterly helpless – my family was falling apart and there was nothing I could do about it. This was really happening. I dashed past the front room but stopped in my tracks when I saw him. It was my brother Andrew; he'd been sat there the whole time. He'd heard everything. His chin was wedged in his hands and he was staring straight ahead.

'Mum's leaving!' I dramatically announced.

'I know,' he replied.

Andrew glanced up at me. His eyes were full of sadness but he didn't say another word. Instead he just turned back and continued to stare straight ahead at the TV, but the screen was all black – it wasn't even switched on.

In the end, it was up to Grandma to come over and calm things down. I don't know who called her or what she said to my parents but at least the shouting stopped.

'Will everything be alright?' I whispered to her later that night as I climbed the stairs to bed. The adults were still in the kitchen talking, their voices quiet and serious. Things were calmer, but I wasn't stupid – I knew the problems were still there.

'Everything will be fine, Katie,' Grandma promised. 'Just get some sleep; you've got school tomorrow.'

The following morning no one spoke at breakfast. We all moved around in our own spaces and ate silently, wrapped up in our own little worlds. Mum and Dad looked as if they hadn't even been to bed. They were both dressed in clothes from the day before and Mum's lovely blonde hair was all mussed up.

'See you later then,' I offered, looking over at them as I grabbed my school bag from the kitchen worktop. When no one replied I shut the door behind me and headed off towards school.

All day long I waited for someone to say something about the clothes flying through the bedroom window at home but no one said a word, not even the bullies. Perhaps I'd imagined it or perhaps it just hadn't gotten out round the neighbourhood yet. Maybe I'd still have a few days' grace before they used it as another weapon to taunt me with.

I confided in Lauren and Megan, although Megan already knew because she lived opposite and had seen the entire thing unfold from her front door.

'So, are they splitting up?' Lauren asked gently.

'I don't know,' I answered. 'But Mum was still there this morning.'

'Well, that's a good sign,' Megan replied.

But I knew it wasn't and I knew it wouldn't blow over as it had before. I'd seen the anger in Dad's eyes. It wasn't just the clothes; it was the way he spoke about Mum to me, as though he hated her. I'd also heard Mum talking to the strange man I now knew was called Phillip, or Phil. The way she'd laughed at something he'd said, as though it was all one big joke. Well, she was the only one laughing and it wasn't even funny.

A few weeks after the big row, I walked in through the front door to find the house cold and silent. I sighed as I hung my coat up and that's when I saw it: a suitcase bunched up close against the wall.

'Katie,' Mum called, 'I'm in here. I need to talk to you.' I gulped. This was it. It was really happening, someone was leaving – the suitcase said it all.

The kitchen was still and silent, there was no smell of cooking, no tea on the boil. The house already felt empty.

As I walked past the suitcase Mum came out to greet me in the hallway.

'Katie,' she said, taking my hands in hers. 'I'm leaving.'

She'd barely got the words out before I began to cry. My whole body crumpled as I took in the news.

'Now then,' Mum said, cradling me in her arms. 'It'll be okay. Look at me,' she said, cupping my weeping face up in her hands. She stared directly at me.

'Everything's going to be alright. We'll all be together again soon, I promise. You hear me, Katie? I said, I promise.'

But her words did little to comfort me. My heart was already broken in two.

'Please don't go, Mum,' I sobbed, the tears welling up, choking in my throat.

Mum wrapped her arms around me and held me tight, like she did when I was a little girl.

'Everything will work out fine, Katie, just you wait and see. You'll still have me and you'll have Dad – we just won't live together anymore. But things will be fine, I promise.'

I wanted to believe her, I truly did, but somehow I knew that things could – and would – never be the same again.

CHAPTER 8

THE FLAT ABOVE
THE SHOP

'Is that you, Katie?' Dad called from the kitchen. I shut the front door behind me.

Every night when I came in from school I was hit by the painful reminder that Mum had gone. She had left us and things were different now.

I called out to him and hung my coat on the usual peg. As I did so, I noticed the empty space where Mum's coat used to hang alongside mine and my heart ached.

Throwing my school bag down in the hall I walked into the kitchen and saw Dad sitting at the kitchen table; his eyes were hollow and sad. He was broken, in more ways than one, but I was only twelve and I didn't know how to fix him.

'I haven't made any tea yet,' he began to say, his voice apologetic.

'Don't worry, I'm not hungry,' I lied as I wrapped my arms around him to give him a hug. I loved Dad more than anything in the world but the truth was, since Mum had gone, our home life was in freefall. Now that she'd left, all the things we once took for granted had vanished along with her. I hated her having this new life without us with her new boyfriend. It transpired that the boyfriend, Phil, had been her first true love. They'd dated as teenagers, split up and lost touch, but one fateful night Mum had gone into town with friends and when she saw the same dark-haired slim man standing at the bar she'd recognised him instantly.

Mum explained it was as if all the years that had passed between them just melted away in that moment. She knew then that she and Phil were meant to be together.

'As soon as we're sorted with a place of our own I'll come for you,' she promised me. I wanted to believe her, but the more the weeks passed, the less I did.

At first Mum and Phil slept in the spare room of a house owned by Phil's friend. I hated the idea of seeing Mum with this strange man, sleeping with him in the same bed in a stranger's house we didn't know. Everything was so alien and unfamiliar.

'We'll all be together soon, just you wait and see,' she promised time and time again over the phone.

I nodded forlornly. I wanted to be with Mum but I also wanted to live with Dad. I wanted it to be the four of us, just as it had always been. But bit by bit, Dad was falling apart. The break-up hit him hard and whilst he tried his best to be there for us, I knew he was struggling. Soon the toll brought him to breaking point. I loved my dad so much and wanted more than ever to make everything alright again, but I didn't know how.

One day, my brother Andrew approached me in the kitchen.

'You know my mate, Dean?' he asked.

I nodded.

'He likes you and wondered if you wanted to go out with him sometime?'

My eyebrows rose before I could stop them. Dean was nice. He was a few years older than me, the same age as my brother, just fifteen, but I felt as though I'd known him forever.

'Really?' I asked, a little surprised.

'So will you then?'

'Will I what?'

'Go out with him?' Andrew sighed.

I thought about Dean. He was tall, good-looking and a good laugh. I could think of nothing I'd rather do than go out with him.

'Okay,' I agreed.

Dean and I met that night and, even though we'd known each other for years, it didn't feel odd when he kissed me. After that, we started hanging around together. I felt happier than I had in ages because I had Dean now. My brother had a girlfriend and the four of us would all hang out together.

If the weather was good, we'd go for a paddle in a nearby lake. It was perfect, sitting in the sunshine, soaking up the rays in Dean's arms.

'I love you, Katie,' he told me, and I believed him. He was my first boyfriend and it felt nice to be loved. It made me feel special.

At first things were perfect. I turned thirteen, and the more time we spent together, the closer we became. But the turmoil at home affected everything including my relationship, and sometimes we'd argue about silly things for no reason. I'd finish it or he would, but our rows were only ever short-lived and within weeks we'd be back together again.

He took things slowly at first but the heavy petting

eventually led to something else. I loved Dean and I wanted him to love me. I thought being a good girlfriend meant having sex with him. I was young and naive but I let my heart rule my head and, when it finally happened, it felt entirely natural and loving. Dean said he cared about me, and he did. He also insisted on using protection although the thought hadn't even crossed my mind.

I didn't worry that I was only thirteen and I'd had sex with a boy. Dean was my boyfriend and he was just fifteen – still a kid himself. We were exploring things together and it felt right. We only had a sex a couple of times but I didn't tell anyone. It was our secret and I loved the idea that someone loved me that much.

One day, after Mum left, she and her new boyfriend Phil came by to pick me up in his car. It was the first time I'd met him properly. I'd seen him in the kitchen that day, of course, but hadn't paid him much attention. But now I was meeting him for real. Mum said they wanted to take me out for the day. I felt guilty spending it with him instead of Dad, but my father was adamant that I maintain contact with Mum.

'Go on,' he said, nudging me towards the door as Phil's silver car pulled up outside. 'Have a great time.'

Dad was smiling but I could see he was hiding his true feelings. He didn't want me to get in that car any more than I did.

'Will you be okay?' I asked, my face crumpled with concern.

'Oh, don't you worry about me,' Dad sighed. 'Now go on, Katie, you don't want to keep them waiting.'

Mum had told me that Phil had a CD player in his car and she'd asked me to bring along my favourite CD. By now, I was really into the American rapper Eminem but although Mum had bought me his CD, I didn't think her stuffy new boyfriend would like it. Instead I randomly picked up a copy of *Now 56* but I was certain Phil wouldn't know anything on it.

I hung my head and approached the car and that's when I saw him – the strange man who'd been at our house that day. He was sitting in the driver's seat with Mum beside him. He was the same age as Dad but he looked younger, with a thick head of black hair. Since the split, Dad had aged overnight. He now looked haunted and old but oddly, Mum looked younger than ever. Her face broke into a huge smile when she saw me.

'Come on, Katie,' she gushed, full of the joys of spring.

I reluctantly pulled open the car door and slid onto the backseat. As I did so Phil spun round to face me.

'Hello, Katie,' he said, smiling warmly as if we'd been friends forever.

But I didn't look up; instead I mumbled a short 'hello'. I didn't want to be friends with this man, no matter how nice he was to me.

The car started up and soon we were on our way.

'We're taking you for a meal,' said Mum, her voice singing with excitement. 'It's a new pub, out of town – I think you'll love it.'

But I didn't want to like it. I just wanted Mum and Dad to be back together and for the four of us to be a family again.

'Okay,' I shrugged. I didn't really care.

'Ooh, did you bring a CD?' Mum asked.

I handed her the CD and Phil slotted it in the player. I rolled my eyes; I didn't want to be there with him. Within seconds the car filled with the sound of the Black-Eyed Peas – another of my favourite bands. But then I heard something else: Phil was singing along and he was word-perfect.

'Do you know this one?' I asked, astonished someone Mum's age could know such trendy music.

'Yeah,' he grinned, cranking up the volume a bit louder, 'it's one of my favourites.'

I flopped back in my seat, flabbergasted.

'Do you know it, Katie?' Phil asked, a moment later.

'Yeah…' I replied, feeling a little stupid. Maybe I'd misjudged him a bit.

'Well, sing along then,' he said, turning up the dial once more, this time to full.

Soon we were all singing along to the music as one song played after the other – Phil knew every word to each song and I was impressed. Maybe Mum's new boyfriend wasn't so bad after all. In the end, we sang all the way to the pub and all the way back home again.

By the time we pulled up outside I was buzzing with excitement but as soon as I saw Dad, I immediately felt guilty that I'd had such a good time without him. He'd been at home waiting for me while I'd been off singing, laughing and joking with Mum and her new boyfriend. I tried to hide my excitement and when he asked if I'd had a good day, I just shrugged.

'It was okay,' I muttered. It had been brilliant but I didn't want to make Dad feel even worse.

Phil changed my mind that day and secretly I thought he was pretty cool. It was good to see Mum happy again and smiling in a way I'd never seen her do at home. But the flip side was Dad and the guilt I felt every time I went out and had a good time without him. It felt like a war between my parents and I was the traitor.

One day, a few weeks later I went over to see Mum and Phil, and she led me into a room crammed full of new things.

'This is all for the flat,' she said, with a span of her hand.

My eyes scanned the room: it was packed full of essentials. There was an ironing board, a kettle, toaster, towels, even a chest of drawers. I thought how odd it was that we had all these things at home but now that she'd left, Mum had had to go out and buy them all over again for her new life. I shuddered. It all seemed so definite. It was as though when she'd bought new linen and towels, she'd bought herself a whole new life too.

'You can come and live with us when we move in,' she promised.

'Okay,' I nodded but I turned away because I didn't want her to see the tears in my eyes.

Two months later, with the new flat secured and a deposit put down, Mum and her boyfriend moved in. Suddenly it was crunch time for me: now I had to decide who I wanted to live with. I felt torn between my parents. Andrew had already decided he would stay with Dad, so I felt as if I had to live with Mum so they could share us out, like possessions.

'Why don't you come and have a look at the flat before you make your mind up?' Mum suggested.

The two-bedroom flat was situated in a modern building directly above a parade of shops. It was a ten-minute drive from my old house but closer to my secondary school, which meant that I wouldn't have to change schools. It was in a different part of town, which was more run-down than the usual neighbourhood I was used to. As Phil parked his car up on the street outside, I noticed how many Asian families there were living in this area. I did a double-take when I saw a beautiful Indian lady dressed in a sari walk by with her two children. They glanced back at us as we climbed out of the car. I looked around and realised why: we were white but we were in the minority here and we stood out because of it. This was an Asian neighbourhood. I'd never been to this area before but Mum and Phil had chosen the flat because it was cheap and all they could afford.

Suddenly I felt butterflies rise in my stomach. Maybe it would be good to live here; maybe it'd be exciting living amongst people from a different culture? Suddenly I began to feel hopeful. None of my friends lived in a flat above a shop but I could. It'd be cool to live on one floor, not in a boring house like everyone else. We'd be able to get take-aways all the time.

'Come on, slow-coach,' Phil called over to me. He took out a small silver key and slid it into the lock of a narrow navy-blue door at the side of the grocery shop. The lock clicked as it turned and the wooden door swung open as if inviting me into the next chapter of my life.

Soon, we were at the top of the stairs and, as I looked around, I spotted the familiar things Mum had bought over the past few months — it was stuff from the room.

'What do you think?' Mum asked, her voice light with excitement.

'Yeah, it's really nice,' I offered.

'But that's not all…come on, follow me,' she said, grabbing at my hand. She led me down a short corridor to another room. I liked the warmth of her hand wrapped around mine and I didn't want her to let go.

'Shut your eyes, Katie,' she said.

I did as I was told; scrunching them up really tight so that I couldn't let any of the surprise in before Mum had a chance to show me. I heard the noise of a door opening and scraping against carpet, which was too long and shaggy on the floor. Mum turned me around. I still had my eyes closed but now I was facing a different direction.

'Open them!' she squealed.

I opened my eyes and gasped. It was a beautiful girl's bedroom filled with lovely new things.

'This is going to be your room,' Mum announced. 'Do you like it?'

I clasped my hand over my mouth to stifle my shriek.

'*Like* it? I love it!'

Mum flung her arms around me and hugged me for all I was worth. I felt so happy that I thought I might burst.

'Look,' she said, leading me across the room. 'There's even a built-in wardrobe.'

She opened a pair of white wooden doors. The wardrobe was massive inside, with plenty of space for all my clothes. There was a new single bed and a bedside table, with an alarm clock and a lamp on top.

A pair of pale pink curtains hung at the window. They matched the new duvet cover, which was pink with cute love hearts scattered all over.

'There's going to be loads of space for all your clothes and your other things, and the best thing is, because we live above a shop, you can play your music as loud as you want because there are no neighbours to hear it!'

I sank down onto the freshly made bed and let the cotton duvet hug my body. Everything was going to be alright.

Mum knew how worried I'd been about moving away from home and leaving Lauren and Megan behind so she'd even arranged for me to meet up with a friend's daughter called Sophie, who lived just round the corner.

'And your friends are welcome to come over here anytime too,' she said, trying to make up my mind.

That night Phil and Mum drove me back to Dad's. As we pulled up outside, Mum had something to ask.

'Katie, you need to make a decision now. Who do you want to live with – me or Dad?'

I felt horrible choosing between them but in my heart I knew my mind was already made up; of course it would be Mum.

Now I'd seen the flat I didn't worry about missing my old friends because I knew that I'd see them every day at school. I was so excited about my new life that I'd almost forgotten the most important person – Dad.

When I walked through the door of my old house, I told Dad my decision. But he didn't say a word; instead he climbed the stairs and went into my bedroom. I didn't know what to do so I followed. When I saw him sitting on my bed I thought my heart would break in two. He was hunched over, staring out into nothingness. Huge tears were streaming down his cheeks and he was clutching my old brown teddy bear in his hands. It was my favourite toy – I'd had him since I was small and he was worn and a little torn around the ears. I loved my bear but I loved my dad more.

But I'd made my decision. Dad's heart had already been broken by Mum, and now I'd broken it just that little bit more.

'Don't forget this,' he said, holding out my teddy in his hands.

But I didn't want my bear, I wanted Dad. I ran to him and wrapped my arms around his big, strong neck. I inhaled the scent of him and tried to hold it in my memory, just in case I forgot what he looked like over the next few weeks.

'I'm sorry…' I began, but I couldn't think of any words to say that would make him feel better.

Dad looked startled. He clasped his hands around my shoulders and held me away from him so that he could look into my eyes.

'Hey, you've done nothing wrong, Katie. I'm just going to miss you, that's all.'

He was just putting a brave face on things but we both knew he was rubbish at it.

Mum told me to go inside and collect my things. I hated packing my clothes into a bag with Dad there but it had to be done and soon I'd have to say goodbye. I felt horrible. I'd thought of nothing else over the past three months. The truth was, I'd wanted to live with both of them but my heart was pulling more towards my mum. Dad had Andrew, Mum didn't. Besides, Dad was struggling to hold down a job, look after us and the house. There were days when I went to school without a packed lunch, or sometimes I'd have to wear a dirty school uniform from the day before because he'd forgotten to put a wash on. I knew it would be easier living with Mum, who'd do all these things for me. It was selfish, but then I reasoned it would be easier on Dad too. He would only have half as much to do without me around.

'Your Mum is coming to get you soon,' he said, his voice cracking with emotion.

'But I don't want to say goodbye,' I replied, hot, frightened tears streaming down my face.

But Dad couldn't speak. He was crying, this time in huge, deep sobs. He gasped for air as the tears came thick and fast. I'd never really seen my father cry before and I didn't know what to do, so I cradled his head in my arms like a baby and just held him there. We remained that way, with me holding Dad and him stroking my hair. Then I heard a familiar car horn toot in the street outside: it was time.

Dad gently prised my arms from him and led me downstairs, holding my hand the whole time. I didn't want him to let go.

Mum was already waiting for me on the doorstep.

'Bye, love,' said Dad, as he held me close one last time. 'Be a good girl for your mum.'

'I will,' I whispered. My voice gave way as emotion over-whelmed me.

'Bye, Dad,' I said, calling to him.

But he wouldn't face me; instead he walked away into the kitchen and out through the back door. He couldn't look back; he couldn't watch me leave.

'Ready?' asked Mum, holding out her hand.

'Ready,' I said. With that I slammed the front door shut and walked up the garden path. I closed the rusty old red gate one last time. I vowed to myself that I'd come and visit Dad once a week. But deep down, now I'd made my choice, I knew things would never be the same again.

Turning the key in the ignition, Phil started up the car engine and soon we pulled away from the house I'd grown up in. I was leaving everything that was once so familiar far behind. I was heading forwards, off to a different and unfamiliar part of town, where we would be the new white people – the odd ones out amongst our Asian neighbours. I tried to convince myself that living in a flat above a shop would be a whole new adventure, something to relish, but as the car wound its way slowly down the street, little did I know how my life would change forever.

CHAPTER 9

MY SECRET 'BOYFRIEND'

'What's your new flat like?' Lauren asked. It was school break and we were sat on the school field, basking in the sunshine.

'It's different, I suppose,' I replied, with a shrug of my shoulders.

Lauren turned; a look of concern clouded her face.

'No, it's cool,' I said, quickly correcting myself.

I didn't want Lauren or anyone else to know how much I missed my old house and Dad. I missed everything about it, my bedroom and my friends. I used to be able to pop round to Lauren or Megan's houses whenever I wanted to. Now, if I wanted to see them, I'd have to organise it well in advance and ask Mum's permission. Everything was wrong. My heart ached for my dad and, when I thought no one was listening, I'd bury my head in my pillow and cry bitterly, soaking it with tears. Life was bearable but only just. With all these people gone, there was a big empty void in my life and I didn't know how to fill it. There were lots of days in the flat when I just felt bored and very alone.

Mum was there, but she was always so preoccupied with Phil and their new life that I sometimes wondered if she even realised I was there. Some nights, although my tea was on the table when I came in from school, I felt as if I was a lodger rather than Mum's daughter. They didn't mean to leave me out but that's how it felt, as if I was living on the edge of their perfect bubble – an outsider, looking in.

The walks home from secondary school were long and lonely too. When I was living at Dad's, I'd walk with Lauren and Megan and we'd chat and sing all the way home. We'd chatter so much that the time would fly and I'd be at my front gates before I even knew it. But now, even though I lived closer to the school, the journey home seemed to drag and take forever. Every time I stepped inside the flat, Mum and Phil would be snuggling up on the sofa together. It made me feel awkward and embarrassed, like a spare part.

A few weeks later, my brother Andrew came to visit. I walked upstairs to find him talking to Mum in the front room of the flat.

'Well, I'm sure we could all squeeze in somehow,' she was saying. 'Maybe the sofa, if that's okay with you?'

Andrew looked either side of him. He was already sitting on the settee.

'Okay,' he agreed. 'I'll bring the rest of my stuff around later tonight.'

I shook my head in disbelief, having heard just enough to work out what was happening.

'But I thought he was living with Dad?' I gasped.

It was the whole reason I'd chosen to live there. Andrew stayed with Dad and I lived with Mum – that was fair, this wasn't.

'Your brother's moving in,' Mum announced, getting to her feet.

'But what about Dad?'

I looked at Andrew but he glanced towards the floor. Mum looked uncomfortable too. I wondered if Dad wasn't coping.

'Your dad will be fine,' Mum snapped. 'It's your brother who's my main priority now.'

'Well, he's not having my room,' I insisted.

'Don't worry. He's on the sofa for now but it's only temporary. When we've got enough money, we'll get a house that's big enough for all of us.'

'But how long's that going to take?' I exclaimed. I missed my old life and I hated the thought of having my big brother living in the front room, sticking his nose into my business.

'As long as it takes,' Mum snapped, beginning to lose her temper. 'Anyway, that's enough! I don't want to hear another word. Andrew's staying here and that's all there is to it.'

My dad was heartbroken when the marriage broke up. He'd mope around the house, looking lost. He was so upset that Andrew was finding it difficult to live there. He missed Mum so it was decided he would live with us. I felt for Dad, he'd done nothing wrong yet he was always the one being punished. The thought of him living alone crippled me with guilt.

The guilt plagued me so much it was all I ever thought of on my walk home from school. One afternoon, I was so caught up in my own thoughts that at first I didn't notice an Asian lad, who appeared to be following me. He trailed the whole way home behind me. It was only when I neared the parade of shops and he stopped to watch me from the other side of the road that I paid him any attention. The following afternoon, the same thing happened again.

I was thirteen years old and although I'd hit puberty a few years before, dressed in my uniform I looked every inch the schoolgirl. I could tell this boy was older than me and wondered what he wanted. He didn't go to the same school and he certainly didn't wear a school uniform. Judging by his hoodie and jeans, I guessed he must have already left. He was tall and well-built, like a man.

The third night I was curious and purposefully looked out for him. Sure enough, as soon as I turned the corner, I spotted him again. My heart raced with excitement as I furtively glanced over. He looked even older than my brother – around eighteen – and when I looked up, I noticed he was smiling back at me. The hood on his top was pulled up close around his face even though it was red hot with the sun beating down. It was odd; although he was hiding from everyone else, he wanted to be seen – by me.

I felt my face flush and looked down at the pavement but as soon as I did, I had the sudden urge to look up again. I couldn't help it – this boy was interested in me. And now he was standing there, leaning against the wall, grinning over.

Suddenly, a thought flashed through my mind: what if he was waiting for someone else? I glanced behind me but there was no one there. I walked along the street but as my step quickened, so did my heartbeat – the lad was following again.

Everything raced through my mind: what if he was a nutter? What if he attacked me? I anxiously looked back again. He'd crossed the road and now he was walking directly behind me. I stopped in my tracks and pretended to tie up my shoelace to see what he'd do. But when I stopped, so did he. I stifled nervous laughter. I wasn't imagining it, he was following me. As I quickened my pace, so did he. By now he was trailing me by a couple of feet. I started to walk again but purposefully stopped and turned in my tracks. He did the same. This time I giggled and he did too. It was comical, as though we were playing a silly game of musical statues. Once more I quickened my pace and he copied me again. This was fun!

I still had a smirk across my face by the time I reached the front door of the flat. This time, like before, the boy hung back. Putting the key in the lock, I glanced over at him one last time and he automatically lifted up the palm of his hand to wave goodbye. It felt odd because I didn't know who he was or what he wanted from me. Yet, despite myself I momentarily lifted my hand and waved back at him. I felt my face flush so I slammed the door before he could see. Afterwards I leant up against the cold wood and I stayed that way for a moment to calm my pounding heart. The adrenalin was still pumping through my veins. Who was the strange boy and what did he want? I was intrigued.

The following day, when the boy was nowhere to be seen, I felt my heart deflate inside my chest. Maybe he'd become bored of me. It was my fault; I should have spoken to him. Maybe because I'd been so rude, I'd never see him again. I hadn't asked this boy to follow me but now that he had, I missed having him around. It gave me something to look forward to – something of my own, a new and delicious secret to keep.

I didn't tell anyone about the boy, not even Lauren or Megan. I don't know why I didn't tell them, maybe it was because I enjoyed the attention and thought if I kept him a secret I'd have him all to myself. Besides, what would I tell them – that a strange Asian boy was stalking me? They'd think that I was making it up. After all, it did sound ridiculous. I even wondered if this mystery man was all in my head – maybe he was a way of escaping my humdrum life?

But when he reappeared the following day, my heart leapt. The sun was high in the sky as I walked through the school gates. Hitching my school bag up on my shoulder, I spotted him as soon as I turned the corner. My whole spirit lifted and I couldn't wipe the smile from my face: he was back and he was there for me. It made me feel special – important. When I coyly caught his gaze and he grinned I felt a flutter in my chest. He was pleased to see me too.

Looking down the street I walked along as normal but this time his pace quickened until I could almost feel his breath on the back of my neck. I held my head high and tried to focus straight ahead but a few minutes later, without warning, the boy crossed over to the opposite side of the road. I wasn't sure what to do; I didn't know if he wanted me to cross over too. Suddenly, I felt young and unsure of myself. I tried to carry on along the street but every so often I glanced over to make sure that he was still there. Now he knew – I was interested in him too. Maybe this was a test?

As we neared the flat, he crossed over to the same side of the road as me and came to an abrupt halt. I turned back because I wasn't sure what to do. As my gaze met his, he gestured over with a simple nod of his head. His eyes were wide and expectant; his hands were thrust deep into his jeans pockets and his hood was pulled up tightly around his face again. Even so, I could tell he looked awkward. He nodded towards me and then to a dirt path which ran around the back of the shops. My heart thudded in my chest. It was obvious what he wanted – he wanted me to follow him.

I glanced up and down the street but I was new to the neighbourhood and there was no one I knew well enough to tell Mum. Apprehensively, I strode towards him. As I did so, he walked up and along the dirt path but kept turning around to check I was still there.

The more he disappeared from view, the more I wanted to follow. Everything told me to stop and run the other way but there was something – something I couldn't see was spurring me on. I wasn't sure if it was curiosity or just sheer stubbornness that wouldn't allow me to turn back. Whatever it was, I needed to know what this boy wanted from me. The dry, dusty dirt puffed up around his feet as he came to a sudden halt up ahead. As I got closer, I saw his face properly for the first time. My heart leapt. He was really good-looking. He wasn't pale and spotty like the boys at school. His skin was a warm, rich amber brown colour. It reminded me of baked sand, exotic spices and faraway lands. He was mysterious and like no one I'd ever met before. I was excited and curious. His eyes stared down at me from underneath the darkened shadow of his hoodie. They were such a deep brown, they were almost black – the colour of precious jet. They shone as, in a low, whispered voice, he began to speak.

'I've noticed you around…' he said in a deep gravelly voice.

My heart fluttered. This good-looking older lad had noticed *me*, not any of the popular girls, just me. I was thrilled. I took a deep breath and tried to steady my nerves. I was young and inexperienced but I didn't want it to show. I wasn't used to boys paying me attention like this.

'*Me*?' I repeated, as though I'd misheard him.

'Yep,' he replied.

In that split second, I studied him. Dressed in his grey hoodie, blue designer jeans and trendy Adidas trainers, I thought how cool he looked. He was older and much more sophisticated than the stupid boys who called me names at school. But why would he notice me? I was plain; I wasn't pretty like the other girls. For a moment, I was worried it was a joke, that someone had put him up to it. But I didn't know him and I was certain he wouldn't know any of the girls at school.

'You live in the flat above the shop, don't you?' he said as more of a statement than a question.

I nodded and swallowed hard. He knew where I lived; he must have noticed me to know something like that.

A silence hung in the air between us. I tried to think of something interesting to say but my mind went blank. I was still trying to think of something when he broke the silence.

'I think you're fit!' he grinned.

I swallowed hard again, it was nerves. I had to stop them and look in control otherwise he'd realise how young and silly I really was. I prayed that he'd not heard me gulp. Suddenly, I felt very inexperienced, standing next to this teenager who was almost a man.

I couldn't believe he'd noticed me and not anyone else. Not one of the girls at school, the ones who always got the boyfriends. No, he'd noticed plain old Katie Taylor, the ugly duckling. The girl they called Dumbo. The girl who everyone thought was rubbish at everything. Here I was standing behind the shops, talking to a good-looking boy who fancied me! He'd followed me and had even picked me out from the crowd. I was special – and I felt it. He'd made me feel like that and I liked it.

'Do you?' I gasped, looking up at him.

My voice sounded as young and immature as the child I actually was. I fiddled with my school tie. The fabric slipped between my fingers as I tried to think of something to say to impress him.

'Yeah, I think you're really fit and I want to see you. Do you want to hang out together?' he asked. He shrugged his shoulders as if I must have been asked the same question every day of my life.

'Yeah, okay,' I answered, a little too quickly; my heart began to thud.

It didn't cross my mind to ask why this older boy would want to hang out with a thirteen-year-old girl. I was just so utterly thrilled and flattered by the attention. At last, I had someone who wanted me because they fancied me, not like my on/off boyfriend Dean – he was just a kid. This boy was cool; he was older and more grown-up. He was gorgeous and he liked me. I lifted my hand and pressed it against the side of my cheek. My face felt hot. I tried to cool it with the back of my hand – I didn't want to look like the nervous, blushing schoolgirl I was.

The boy smiled and cupped my face with his hand, it felt nice.

'Have you got a mobile?' he asked.

'Yeah,' I gasped, my fingers fumbling deep down in my school bag to show him. I held it up in mid-air as if to prove it.

'Great, give me your number, then I can text you.'

I told him my number and he tapped it quickly into the keypad.

'Er, what's your name?' he asked suddenly.

'Katie,' I replied, unable to wipe the grin off my face. 'Katie Taylor.'

'Katie,' he grinned. 'Nice name.'

I swallowed my nerves and watched as he keyed in my name and stored it on his mobile phone. I could hardly believe this was happening.

'Right, Katie, I'll call you, okay? Keep your phone near you so you can see when I text you. Have you got credit on it?'

'Yep,' I nodded.

'Great, well, I'll call you soon. And remember, keep your phone with you.'

I smiled back at him. It was a big, soppy grin but I couldn't help it or wipe it from my face. I was beside myself with excitement. Saying goodbye, I ran back along the dirt path towards the shops and the flat. My head was light and my heart so full of joy I thought it would burst. This boy had left school, he was all grown up, almost an adult, yet he fancied me.

I bet he could have any girl he wanted, yet he wants me, I thought smugly to myself as I turned the key in the lock. I wished I could have seen the girls' faces at school – this would shut them up!

Mum was upstairs making a cup of tea as I reached the top of the flat stairs. Phil had his hands on her waist, the way my dad used to, and he was nuzzling small kisses into the side of her neck. She batted him away but all too soon she let him do it again and she squealed with joy when he did. Normally, I hated seeing them kiss like this but today I didn't mind because today, something good had happened to me. I had a secret but, I decided, I wouldn't tell a soul – this was mine to keep.

Today, I'd got myself a boyfriend and not just any boyfriend, this was a gorgeous older boy and he fancied me. Then I realised something: I didn't even know his name.

CHAPTER 10

SCHOOL, SPLIFFS AND SELF-HARM

'I've just realised, I never told you my name,' the voice said on the other end of the line. It was the boy I'd met behind the shops, the one who said he'd fancied me.

'No,' I replied, trying to hide the excitement in my voice. I was sitting in my bedroom, whispering into my mobile so that Mum and Phil wouldn't hear. I wanted to keep my secret boyfriend just that – a secret.

'It's Sarim,' he replied.

I formed the word with my mouth and, in a silent whisper, I repeated it over and over to myself.

'But my friends call me Sam for short,' he added.

'Are you still at school?'

'Oh no,' Sam replied, 'I left a few years ago. I'm eighteen now and I work in a restaurant.'

I was impressed. Not only was my secret boyfriend loads older than all of my friends, he also earned his own money.

'Wow!' I gasped.

'Listen,' said Sam, 'do you want to meet up sometime so we can hang out together?'

I could think of nothing else I'd rather do.

'That'd be great!'

'Good, I'll call you tomorrow then. Okay?'

'Yep,' I replied. I liked the fact he was older, that he made decisions and took control. Not like Dean; he was still a kid.

'See you then.' Sam said and he hung up.

I pressed 'end call', held the phone against my chest and tried to steady my racing heart. I had a secret boyfriend and he was nothing like the other boys at school I knew. I was mesmerised. Sam was cool and grown up *and* he had a job! My whole body felt light. I didn't really know what love was but I was beginning to wonder if this was it.

The following night I ran straight home from school. I lay on my bed with my mobile at the side of me, watching it, waiting for it to light up and ring. Around 5pm it did.

'I'm outside behind the shops – see you in a minute,' he said.

Pushing the phone into the back pocket of my jeans, I grabbed a hoodie and made for the door.

'Where are you going?' Mum asked. She was in the kitchen, stirring something in a pan.

'I'm just going to call for Sophie, to see if she's in.' I lied.

Mum nodded approvingly. She'd been worried I'd not made any friends at the flat, so if I said I was meeting Sophie, I knew it'd keep her off my back for a while.

'Okay, good. Don't be long, though – your dinner will be ready in less than an hour.'

'Okay,' I yelled as I dashed downstairs to the door and the street below.

Sam was waiting for me when I ran up the dirt path.

'Nice hoodie,' he said, nodding in approval. I'd chosen it especially because I knew he was trendy and it was the coolest thing I owned.

'Thanks,' I said, a little breathless from all the running.

For the next hour Sam asked me about myself and how I'd ended up living above a shop.

'It's complicated,' I sighed, and I began to explain all about Mum, Dad and Phil. Sam sat on the wall and listened intently to everything I said. He asked me questions too, as though he was really interested. It felt good to have someone to talk to, someone who was interested.

'How about you?' I asked, realising that I'd hijacked the entire conversation.

But he shrugged. It was clear he didn't want to talk about himself or his family.

The time flew by and when I finally glanced down at my watch, I realised that I'd already been longer than an hour.

'Sorry, Sam,' I panicked. 'I've got to go, I'm really late.'

'Okay,' he sighed, jumping down from the wall, 'but I'll see you again, won't I?'

My heart leapt with joy.

'Yeah, of course,' I mumbled, flushing bright red at the attention.

Sam leaned in and put his hand around the back of my head. Soon our lips were touching as he kissed me. Other than Dean, it was the first time I'd been properly kissed and I felt unsure of myself because Sam was older. I was worried I'd do something wrong and look stupid. I didn't want Sam to think I was an idiot schoolgirl because I didn't feel like that when I was with him, I felt special and kind of grown up.

Moments later, he pulled away.

'You better go; you don't want to get into trouble,' he smirked, giving me a playful shove.

'See you tomorrow?' I asked hopefully.

'Sure.'

I turned and ran back home.

The following night we talked some more but this time we kissed for longer. I didn't even mind when Sam eased his hand up inside my top and felt under my bra. This was what boyfriends and girlfriends did; this was normal.

I wanted to tell Lauren. She was my best friend and we didn't keep secrets from one another but it was obvious that Sam hadn't told anyone about me because he wouldn't tell me anything about himself. He was a closed book, so I guessed he'd want to keep us a secret too.

A week or so later, I met him in the usual spot. His face lit up when I approached. It made me feel good. Suddenly, he pulled a large bunch of keys out from his back pocket and dangled them in front of my face.

'What are they?' I asked.

'Keys to the restaurant. Do you want to come with me? It'll be more private there.'

'Okay,' I shrugged.

I knew it'd be good to spend time somewhere nicer than the dirt path. A restaurant sounded lovely, romantic even. But first, Sam had some instructions for me. He'd set off, walking ahead, and I would follow but I couldn't get too close to him in case people guessed we were together.

'I'm not allowed to date white girls,' he said by way of explanation.

'Okay,' I agreed, but part of me felt a little put out. I

wondered if he was ashamed to be seen with me. But I loved Sam and I wanted to make him happy so I shook the negative thoughts from my head.

Ten minutes later, after trailing through street after street, we reached the back of another parade of shops. Sam walked down a narrow alleyway and stopped at a black metal door. Finally, with a wave of his hand, he signalled over to me and beckoned me forward.

'Over here,' he whispered.

I dashed over to him and slipped in quickly through the metal door at the back of the restaurant. Once inside Sam closed the door tight and reached up above my head and slid a thick metal bolt across the top of it.

'There,' he said, turning to face me, 'nice and private.'

He leaned in for a kiss and I giggled as I felt his mouth against my neck. His hands were roaming under my clothes and up and down my body but I didn't mind. This was love and I was smitten with Sam; he was everything I wasn't. He was sophisticated, good-looking and cool. I imagined the nasty girls and what they'd say if they saw me kissing this older boy. They'd be green with envy.

Soon, one thing had led to another and when Sam undid my jeans, I let him. Before long he'd undone his jeans too.

'Do you know what a blow job is?' he asked.

I covered my mouth and began to giggle. I knew what one was but I felt embarrassed.

'Here,' he said, guiding my head down to his crotch, 'I'll teach you how to do it.'

I was thirteen, and I knew I shouldn't be doing things like this with a lad I hardly knew, but Sam was different. He was my boyfriend; he was kind and loving. He called me 'babe' and he made me feel like one. He called me gorgeous, sexy and beautiful and told me I was special. I loved hearing those words. They made me feel good. I was still seeing Dean but our relationship seemed so immature compared to the one I now had with Sam. He was the real deal. I couldn't help it; I knew I was falling in love with him. He made me feel older, sexy even, not like some stupid schoolgirl. With him I could leave my old life behind.

After we'd had oral sex, Sam sat down and pulled out a roll-up cigarette from his jacket pocket.

'Do you know what this is?' he asked, grinning as he played with the thin white cig between his fingertips.

'A joint?' I guessed.

'Yeah, that's right. It's a joint. Have you ever had one before?'

I nodded. I hadn't smoked a full joint but one of my brother's friends had once let me have a puff on one when Dad was out. My parents would have gone crackers if they knew but I never told them and I knew that Andrew wouldn't either.

'Here,' Sam said, handing me the joint, 'Have some, it'll relax you.'

As I inhaled the smoke I felt a sense of calm envelop me as if every muscle in my body had been switched off and tuned into chill-out mode. We smoked the joint, passing it between us until it was just a stub in my fingertips. Sam noticed and took out another one. He lit it and we smoked that one too.

Afterwards, my head swam and my body felt so light that I was certain I could float. Sam watched as my eyes rolled back in my head. He lifted me up onto a metal worktop and laid me down on top of it. He pulled out a condom from his pocket and rolled it on himself. His body felt hot and firm as he rested his weight upon me and we began to have sex. I was so stoned that I don't remember much more about my first time with

Sam. But I didn't care: Sam was a man and I still couldn't believe that someone like him would fancy me.

When he'd finished, Sam jumped to his feet and dressed himself. He must have helped me put my clothes on again because as I came round, I realised that I was almost fully dressed again. He seemed in a rush.

'I'll take care of you,' he said, finally caressing me in his big strong arms. 'Do you hear me, Katie?' he repeated. 'I'll take care of you.'

I believed him. That's what I loved about Sam; he was the only person who wanted to take care of me. Sure, Mum fed me when I came in from school but she was so wrapped up in her new life that I doubt she'd have even noticed if I wasn't there. I loved my dad but I hardly ever saw him now. Occasionally he would text or call me, and he'd come to the flat but it was always awkward because we'd have to stand outside talking. It felt uneasy, stilted and odd.

But Sam was different: he made me feel wanted and gave me the attention I so desperately craved. A few days later, when he told me that he loved me, I thought I'd burst with pure joy because I loved him too. I dreamed we'd get married and be together forever. I'd be Sam's wife and everyone would look up to us, but for the moment I was enjoying the sensation of being in love. I realised this was what had been missing from my life – love. For the first time I felt complete, just like everyone else: I fitted in.

A few days later I was at school, struggling to keep up in a computer lesson, when one of the popular girls, Deborah, noticed.

'Hey, look at Dumbo!' she crowed, causing the others to turn and stare.

'Shut up,' I shouted back. I had Sam now, I wasn't afraid of anyone anymore.

'You can't do it 'cos you're thick!' she jeered.

The whole class started to pick on me, with Deborah acting as ringleader.

'Well, at least I'm not fat, like you!' I hissed. The words left my mouth before I had a chance to think what I was saying.

Deborah rose up from her seat. The others watched open-mouthed as she strode over towards me. Bending down to look at me square-on, she pressed her face in front of mine.

'You wanna watch your back,' she sneered, "cos I'll be waiting for you at the school gates.'

I shrugged my shoulders as if I didn't care but inside I was terrified. My stomach twisted in knots throughout the rest of the lesson. I dreaded the end of the day because I knew she'd be there.

Later that day, when I approached the school gate, a boy whizzed past me on his bike. He turned and broke sharply until he was blocking my exit.

'You can't go through,' he insisted.

'Yes, I can,' I said, trying to shove past him. But he inched forward until his bike was right across the school gate.

'You can't pass until you've spoken to Deborah.'

My heart lurched. I looked behind the boy and spotted her. She was surrounded by a bunch of girls; they'd been waiting for me.

I was totally alone. I gulped back my nerves and kept my head down as I tried once more to walk through the gate.

'No you don't,' Deborah said, standing in my way. 'You haven't said sorry.'

I looked up at her. 'For what?'

'For what you said earlier.' She turned back to the crowd gathering behind her.

Then I felt a hand against my chest as she shoved me hard. I fell backwards.

'Nope,' she decided, 'you can't pass until you've said sorry.'

The crowd started to laugh and I felt stupid. I didn't want to say sorry; I wanted to get home so that I could be with Sam. The thought of seeing him was the only thing that kept me going.

'Sorry,' I mumbled the word so quietly that I could barely hear myself.

'What did you say?' Deborah's voice boomed jubilantly. 'Repeat it loud enough so we can all hear.'

I looked directly into her eyes. She was a big, tough girl and she wasn't someone to be messed with. My nerves jangled with fear.

'Sorry,' I stammered.

'That's better,' she sneered, 'but now you have to say "please" if you want to get past. In fact, you've got to say "pretty please",' she snorted. The others laughed along too.

But I didn't want to say 'please' or 'thank you'. I didn't want to beg. I wasn't the pathetic old Katie anymore; I was the confident, grown-up one and I had Sam. If I didn't stand up to her, I knew she'd do it again and again. I turned to face her head on.

'Get out of my way,' I demanded. I was so fired-up that my fist clenched as I spoke.

'What did you say?' Deborah asked, her eyes widening.

She wasn't used to anyone answering back. I shook a little when I noticed her body stiffen at the thought of a confrontation.

'I said, get out of my way…now.' I couldn't back down now.

'Ooh, I'm really frightened,' she whined. 'Everyone's scared of Katie Taylor; everyone's scared of the freak!'

I'd had enough. Even though my whole body was quivering with fear I tried to push her aside but it was no good, she was built like a brick wall – I didn't stand a chance.

'Don't you dare,' she said, smacking me in the face.

Her fist thudded hard against the side of my cheek and I bent over double as the pain set in.

'That's what you get for being a freak – a Dumbo!' she laughed.

But something inside snapped.

'Well, at least I'm not a fat cow like you!' I screamed.

Everyone gasped and watched as Deborah pulled back her arm. Her fist sailed down on me, striking the side of my head. Pain ripped through my body but I knew I had to fight back. I punched her as hard as I could, catching her in the mouth. It momentarily knocked her off-balance then I noticed her dabbing something on her bottom lip. The force had split it open and now there was blood all over her fingertips. As soon as she saw it she went crazy, like a woman possessed.

'Right, that's it,' she said, slinging her bag on the floor, 'you asked for this!'

I felt the dirt in my mouth as she pushed my face hard against the dry bare ground.

'Eat dirt, that's all you're good for, you fucking freak!'

The crowd cheered her and jeered me.

'Freak, freak, freak!' they chanted in unison, their voices rising.

I squirmed and wriggled enough to break from her grasp but as I tried to fight back a cracking pain to the left-hand side of my face floored me. I felt my cheekbone crack as a dead weight crunched against it: it was her fist. She smacked me again, this time near the side of my eye; it swelled almost immediately. My head throbbed and my face ached with pain. I felt as though I'd just been hit by a truck. I wanted this to be over with but there was more to come. Blow after blow rained down. I tried to fight back but she was bigger and stronger than me, and egged on by her gang of mates, it was as though she had the strength of ten men. Finally, after what seemed like an eternity, she stepped away and dusted herself down.

'Don't you ever, *ever* speak to me like that again, understand?' she screamed.

I nodded weakly. I felt sick and dizzy with pain.

Deborah snatched up her bag from the floor.

'Ugly bitch! No one likes you and they never will. We all hate you 'cos you're a fucking *freak*!'

She turned and marched off with her friends in tow.

Humiliation flooded through me. Slowly, I picked myself up and dusted my clothes down. I'd seen the crowd and I knew that by first thing tomorrow morning, the whole school would know. Just as my life had started to go well, something had to come along and ruin it. I thought of Sam and my heart ached – I wished he was here now. He'd take care of me, just as he promised. He was my boyfriend – he'd protect me.

My face was sore. It felt puffy and swollen in my hands. I didn't have to see myself to know I looked a complete mess. I didn't want Sam or anyone else to see me like this but I knew I'd have to go home.

'What's happened to your face?' Mum gasped as soon as I walked in the flat. 'Oh my God!' she said, covering her mouth as she inspected the damage.

'Phil, *Phil*!' she screamed. Phil came running through in a panic.

'It's Katie,' she said, 'she's been attacked.' Mum hopelessly dabbed at my wounds with a tissue. It made me flinch.

'Katie,' she said, grabbing me by the shoulders. 'You've *got* to tell me – who did this to you?'

I staggered over to the sofa, sank down onto it and then I began to cry. I told her all about the girl at the gate and a bit about the bullying I endured on a daily basis. Mum sat beside me and listened to everything.

'Right, that's it!' she said, jumping to her feet, 'I'll see what the Headmaster has to say about this!'

She grabbed the phone and angrily punched in the number.

'No, Mum, *don't*!' I begged. I knew the phone call would make things ten times worse.

'I don't care,' Mum insisted 'She's not getting away with this. Look at the state of your face,' she said, resting her hand against her throat to catch the sob rising inside.

Someone answered on the other end of the line and Mum asked to be put through to the Headmaster. She started arguing down the phone with the secretary and wouldn't take no for an answer.

'This is important, you'll put me through now!' she said in a voice I'd never heard before.

Mum eventually spoke to the Head, who promised to look into it, but I didn't expect much to be done: the bullies ran the school, not him. After the call, Deborah was disciplined and suspended for a week. Mum wanted the police to take action but because the girl was the same age as me, all they could do was give her a caution.

I knew she'd been punished but the attack shattered what

little confidence I had. I refused to return to school despite reassurances from the Headmaster. I felt depressed and wanted to hide away from everyone, including Sam.

'I've been grounded,' I lied, when he called soon afterwards.

'What for?' he asked.

'Fighting,' I replied.

I told him all about Deborah, although I didn't tell him the names she and the other kids had called me – I didn't want to put him off me.

'How long are you grounded for?' he asked.

'A week, at least,' I whispered.

'Must have been some fight!' he laughed.

'It was. But I promise I'll see you soon. I'll text you, Sam, promise.'

I hated not being able to see him – I felt as if I was being punished. I worried he'd get bored and go off with someone else. But I needn't have – Sam did wait and when he agreed to meet me once more, I felt so utterly grateful to him.

But I refused to go back to school. The swelling eventually subsided but the bruises took longer to disappear. Lauren, Megan and Beth sympathised but that's all they could do; they were as frightened of Deborah as I was. In the end, it was a month before I went back and, when I did, Deborah was sitting in my form class. I hoped they'd move her but they didn't. As soon as I saw her, my heart began to pound with terror. I knew she'd had a caution and wouldn't dare touch me but she also had mates – lots of them.

'Look who's back,' one sneered when they saw me hovering by the classroom door. It took all the strength I had just to walk in and sit down at my desk.

After that, Deborah left me alone but the threat of violence was always there. It hung in the air. I knew I'd be punished again, but I didn't know when or where it would be.

When I finally met Sam he took me to the restaurant. I was so glad to see him that I let him have sex with me again and again. This time he'd brought along some alcohol – WKD Blue. It became my favourite. I loved the sweet taste, like cherryade. As the drugs and alcohol gripped my body, I believed this light, relaxed feeling was love but it wasn't really. I was high. And when I was high I lost control of my inhibitions and allowed Sam to do all kinds of things to me. Sexually, nothing was out of bounds.

'I've missed you,' I said, snuggling my head into his big strong neck.

'Yeah,' he replied coldly. My heart dive-bombed. It was clear that Sam hadn't missed me quite as much as I'd missed him.

'You do love me, don't you?' I asked, the words sounding stupid and childish as soon as I'd spoken them.

Sam took a huge drag on the spliff between his fingertips. He shrugged and looked down at the ground but he wouldn't answer me.

'Don't you love me?' I asked, feeling more stupid by the minute.

I angrily fastened my bra and pulled down my top. I couldn't explain it but his reaction made me feel cheap and unloved. Still, Sam said nothing.

'Right,' I huffed, jumping down off the worktop. I fastened the top button of my jeans and blinked back the tears pricking behind my eyes. 'If that's what you think of me…'

'Hey,' Sam soothed, wrapping a lazy arm around my shoulder. 'It's just a bit of fun, that's all, Katie.'

'So you don't love me?' I huffed, folding my arms across my

chest. I needed some reassurance and I wanted it now. Sam realised and snaked his arms around my waist. He pulled me close but I resisted – I didn't want him to think he had it all his own way. I pulled a childish face, a scowl, as if I didn't believe him.

'Of course I love you, that's why I'm with you. I've told you, Katie, I'm gonna take care of you, I promise. Hey,' he said, suddenly changing the subject, 'do you wanna see some pictures?'

'Of what?'

Sam grabbed his mobile from the back pocket of his jeans and pulled up different images of cars on the screen.

'This one's my favourite,' he said, his eyes misting over.

I looked but it was just a car to me, it meant nothing. One by one, he flicked through different images of cars. They were all racer-boy cars, souped-up things with big wheels and fancy engines.

'One day, I'll have one just like that,' he insisted, pointing at the screen.

But I wasn't interested. I didn't care what car he drove – I loved Sam for who he was, not what he had.

'See this?' he said, turning the phone screen towards me again. But I didn't bother to look because it'd be just another car.

'That's my gun,' he said suddenly.

I stopped in my tracks and glanced at the screen. I saw a photograph of a black handgun. Now he had my full attention.

'A *gun*?' I said, as I pulled the phone closer to get a better look.

Sam grinned as I stared harder at the screen: it was a picture of a gun. I suddenly felt frightened. Then it dawned on me, I didn't really know Sam at all. Maybe I'd got involved with someone who was in trouble. Maybe he was in a gang – that would explain all the drink and drugs he gave me.

'Is it…is it *real*? Is it really yours?' I asked, trying to hide my shock.

Sam nodded. I was stunned. I thought I knew Sam but deep down, I realised I didn't know anything about him at all. Whenever I asked questions he'd refuse to answer. I was thirteen, but he was eighteen – a grown man. He wanted flash cars and had a picture of a gun on his phone – *his* gun, he said. I wasn't sure if I believed him but then, I wasn't sure what to believe anymore. The thought stayed with me from that moment on. Maybe Sam was dangerous; maybe he was a bad person who was involved with dangerous things and dangerous people. Or, maybe he was making it all up, just to impress me? Yes, I convinced myself. That was it. It could be a picture from anywhere – a toy gun even. I was just a kid, I wouldn't know the difference.

But something changed that day and I realised for the first time that I was a little out of my depth. He was older than me and he moved in grown-up circles. I felt naive and foolish. However much I tried to convince myself otherwise, the seed of doubt had been planted in my mind. I knew nothing about Sam, his background or his family – I didn't even know where he lived. But he knew everything about me. He had sex with me in the back of a restaurant when he knew that no one was around. I didn't even know how he got hold of the keys. Maybe he'd stolen them?

Then it dawned on me: every time we met he expected sex. At first he'd been gentle but now he didn't even bother being nice. He brought drugs and alcohol but always expected something in return. That's what I was there for, so that he could have sex with me in the back of a restaurant. Things shifted for me and it was as though I was seeing things clearly for the very first time. Having sex in the kitchen of a restaurant wasn't loving at all; it was dirty and seedy. I started to wonder if Sam had ever loved me or if he'd just been using me all this time.

One night I decided to challenge him. Did he want me or did he just want sex?

When he began to paw at my body I pushed him away.

'Not tonight,' I insisted, 'can't we just…I don't know, can't we just talk or something?'

I sat back on the worktop and buttoned up my top, but Sam wasn't happy.

'Talk? We *always* talk!' He started to shout. 'What do you want to talk about?' he said, waving his arms around in a temper.

I could tell he was pissed off with me. He made me feel like I was wasting his time. The expression on his face changed and his eyes narrowed. I started to feel a little frightened but Sam began to laugh.

'I just want to talk, Sam, that's all,' I sighed but he laughed louder and louder. I didn't understand. He was laughing to himself like he was crazy. It frightened me.

He jumped to his feet and walked over to the door. Stretching up, he reached for the bolt at the top. It was already locked from the inside but he slid the bolt across too. I ran over and tried to unlock it, but I couldn't get out; I was trapped. I looked up at Sam but he was still laughing and then it hit me: he was laughing at me.

'I want to go home,' I said, my voice beginning to shake.

'No. You're not leaving here until we have sex,' he insisted. He shoved me away from the door.

'Let me out, right now!' I demanded.

'Nope,' he smirked, 'not until you have sex with me.'

But I didn't want to have sex with him. I just wanted to talk but Sam had locked me in. I was trapped and I knew he wouldn't let me go until I'd had sex with him. I was simply terrified.

'I'm tired, I want to go home. Please let me go,' I begged.

Sam nodded and for a moment I thought he'd changed his mind. But as soon as I began to relax, I spotted a sickly smirk spreading across his face.

'Okay, have sex with me and then I'll let you go.'

I didn't know what to do. I thought Sam was my boyfriend and I thought I loved him but now I didn't feel love, only fear. I was trapped and he was forcing me to do something I didn't want to do. I felt scared and unsure. I'd never been in a situation like it before, and I suddenly realised how stupid I'd been. I'd gotten myself into this mess and I knew there was only one way out. I had no choice – I'd have to do as he said.

With the back door of the restaurant secure from prying eyes, he strode back over and pulled me roughly towards him. I was angry because I didn't want to do it but I felt weak and powerless. There was no way out: I'd have to have sex with Sam so that I could go home.

As he laid his body on top of mine, I turned my head to the side so that he wouldn't see my tears. I'd never been frightened of him before, but I was now. I didn't want to do it but he made me anyway. It was uncomfortable and, for the first time, it hurt. Afterwards, he told me how much he loved me but I didn't believe him anymore. I was only thirteen years old, but I was old enough to know that you didn't do things like that to someone you loved.

Later that night, I took the pencil sharpener out of my

pencil case. I had a full day at school the next day and I just couldn't face it — a full day of name calling and intimidation between classrooms.

Sliding my thumbnail into the groove of the screw of the blade, I turned it so that it came undone. I couldn't believe how easy it was to part the blade from the sharpener. I held the thin metal between my fingers. It caught the light, the silver metal glinting back at me as if it was daring me to do my worse. Clutching the blade between my finger and thumb, I rolled up the sleeve on my right wrist and sliced the hard metal edge against my skin. The blade was so sharp that at first, I didn't even feel the pain. A thin red crimson stripe immediately peeked across and then oozed from my wrist. As soon as I saw it, I immediately felt better. Even though the pain had started to throb, the sight and colour of my blood spurred me on, urging me to cut again and again. They were just surface cuts but deep enough to draw enough blood and it felt good. Every time another crimson stripe appeared it was as though I'd been greeted by an old friend. It made me feel better because for the first time, I felt in control. I realised this was something I could do — I'd just found a way to release all the pain and anger I'd bottled up inside.

After that night, when the bullying or constant demands for sex became too much, I'd draw the blade across my skin. Soon my arm was a network of tiny cuts. I looked as if I'd punched my way through a pane of glass but only I knew the truth. Like my boyfriend Sam, I kept my scars hidden — they were two secrets I had to keep and I wouldn't ever tell anyone or let them see.

Soon I was harming myself almost every night. My right arm was sore and bloodied but it didn't matter because it was worth it. The pure and utter relief it gave in return made me feel like new again. The urge to harm was now so strong that I became addicted to it. Like a drug, the urge was there all the time. Sometimes I fought against it but in the end, I'd relent and pull out the same blade. In many ways the blade had become my best friend and confidant. When it was just the two of us, I knew I would always feel better.

Both Sam and the school bullies had complete control over me but when that blade was in my hands I had control, and I liked it.

I thought life had become unbearable – it was a merry-go-round of abuse, mental, physical and sexual. But worse was yet to come.

CHAPTER 11

THE CORNER SHOP

After a year of living in the flat above the shop, Mum and Phil had some news. They'd found a house for us all to live in. Andrew was delighted because it meant he wouldn't have to sleep on the sofa anymore. There was only one problem: the new house was half an hour's walk away from the flat and a couple of miles from Sam. We'd been seeing each other for six months but I knew we'd have to split up.

I thought Sam would be upset when I told him but he didn't seem bothered.

'I'll text you,' he said coldly.

I said I'd come back and see him but I didn't mean it, not really. I'd been wary of him since the night he'd forced me to have sex with him in the back of the restaurant. Then there was the gun. I believed it was his and I sensed there was a side to him I really didn't know. In a way, the move would be my escape – a new beginning.

Afterwards, I made a couple of half-hearted journeys over to the other side of town to meet him but eventually things just fizzled out. In many ways I felt relieved. I received the occasional text from him but I knew it'd had been a fling and now it was over.

Then, not long after we moved, I realised another girl walked home from school the same way as me. Her name was Vicky and soon we became inseparable. One day we were on our way home when it started to pour with rain.

'I'm soaked!' Vicky shrieked, holding her bag above her head to stop her hair from getting wet. Neither of us was wearing a coat and within minutes we were soaked through to the skin.

'Quick,' she squealed. 'Let's go in here and get warm.'

She ran into a nearby shop with me close behind. The shop was warm inside. I'd passed it before but I'd never been in; it was a general store selling tinned food, newspapers, sweets and cigarettes.

'I'm starving,' Vicky gasped. She searched in her school bag for loose change and pulled some out. 'I'm having a bag of crisps, want some?'

I nodded but as I did so I noticed a chubby Asian man standing in the background behind the counter, watching us.

Vicky grabbed the crisps and headed towards him. Taking the money from her hand, he keyed the amount into the till and it beeped loudly. As we turned to leave, he looked up at me and smiled. I thought he was just being friendly so I smiled back but as I walked out of the door I turned to face him again, only this time he winked. I thought it was odd but it made me laugh.

A few days later, we called at the shop again. Soon we were calling there two or three times a week. Each time, the man's face would light up as soon as he saw us. He'd smile and wink at me but it made me laugh because he was old enough to be my dad.

After a few weeks, he started talking to us. Lighting a cigarette up behind the counter, he told us his name.

'I'm Wadi,' he said, taking my hand and shaking it. 'What are your names?'

'I'm Katie and this is Vicky,' I replied, pointing at my friend. She suddenly remembered the bag of crisps she was holding in her hand and went to pay him.

'No, no,' Wadi said. 'No need to pay. Have that on me.'

'But won't your boss mind?' I asked.

'No,' he grinned. 'Because I am the boss – this is my shop.'

'Oh right,' I said. I felt a bit silly now: it was obvious, that's why he was allowed to smoke.

I guessed Wadi was in his thirties but the extra weight he was carrying made him look even older. He was scruffily dressed, wearing a stained dark shirt, which strained across his belly. He also had badly-dyed black hair. Wadi told us he'd owned the shop for a few years and he ran it along with two family friends called Tali and Rafan.

'But I'm in charge,' he said, proudly puffing out his chest. The buttons on his shirt strained even more.

We spent the next ten minutes talking. Wadi already knew our names but now he wanted to know where we lived. I told him all about my recent move from the flat to the house. He nodded intently as I spoke and even made us a cup of tea. He was nearer my dad's age than mine, but I thought how kind he was. As he placed the mugs down on the counter, he dipped down and I spotted a small bald patch at the back of his head. He'd combed his thinning hair over in a bid to disguise it but that just made it more obvious. I thought it was sad that he was trying so hard to keep young.

'You girls drop in anytime you like,' he insisted as we finally turned to leave.

After that day, whenever we called in Wadi would give us free cigarettes and sweets.

'Help yourselves,' he insisted, holding out a packet of cigs. Vicky and I grabbed at them greedily. They cost a fortune and neither of us ever had enough money to buy them.

One day when we called, Wadi's colleague Tali was there. He moved around in the background, silently stacking shelves, but he watched us the whole time. Unlike Wadi, Tali was slim and better-looking and I fancied him. Every time he caught my eye, he'd wink. I was flattered because it was obvious that he liked me and it made me feel special. Even though I still had an on/off relationship with Dean, after Sam I'd decided that I liked the attention of an older man.

Wadi walked in from the back of the shop. He was delighted to see us.

'My girls!' he announced, throwing his hands up in the air like we were old friends. 'I've missed you both! Come in, come in.'

He waved us over and pulled up two chairs behind the counter. Vicky giggled and shot me an excited look. He always made us feel so important – important enough to sit behind the counter. Wadi leant against it, resting his elbows on top of a pile of newspapers. His eyes never left us for a second as he began to ask more questions.

'You don't need to tell me which school you go to, I can tell,' he said, gesturing towards our school ties.

'So, how old are you both?'

'Fourteen,' we chorused in unison.

We heard ourselves and burst out laughing because we sounded as young as we were. Wadi smiled. He ran a hand through his thinning hair and stood up but he didn't take his eyes off me once. My face flushed. It was obvious he liked me. I liked him too, but not in that way; I liked him because he was kind. Unlike the other kids, we didn't need money in his shop – we could have anything we wanted for free. All we had to do was ask.

'Help yourself to chocolate,' he urged. 'There's plenty more in the back, isn't there, Tali?'

Tali put down the price gun he was holding in his hands and nodded. He looked directly at me and smiled as he spoke.

'You girls are welcome in here anytime.'

I studied him for a moment. Unlike Wadi, Tali had naturally thick dark hair which shone a blue-black colour in the light. His eyes were wide and his mouth was plump. He was good-looking, much better-looking than Wadi. He caught me staring so I averted my eyes and stared down at the ground, but Wadi noticed too.

The next day we were in the shop when Wadi called me over. He was standing alone behind the counter.

'I have something very important to ask you,' he whispered, looking over my shoulder to see where Vicky was, but she was at the back of the shop. It was obvious this was a message just for me.

'I want your phone number.'

'Why?' I replied. I wondered why Wadi wanted my number and not Vicky's.

'Because I want to chill out with you, spend time with you. You are beautiful and sexy, Katie, and I like talking to you,' he gushed.

I blushed because I was flattered. Even though he was fat and unattractive, it didn't matter because Wadi thought I was prettier than Vicky. I gave him my mobile number.

'We can hang out together,' he said, putting a finger to his lips as if this was our secret.

I didn't tell Vicky or anyone else. I don't know why, I just thought things like this were best kept secret.

The following day, Vicky was off school so I walked home alone. I thought about calling in at the shop but something stopped me. An hour later, I was at home when my phone rang – it was Wadi.

'Meet me at the shop,' he begged.

'Now?' I gasped. I'd only just got changed out of my school uniform.

'Yes, I've shut the shop. It's quiet and I'm all alone – I'm bored. I just want to chill with you because you're beautiful and sexy.'

I blushed again. Even though Wadi was old enough to be my dad, I liked it when he said nice things like that – it made me feel special.

'But what will we do?' I said. I felt a little unsure without my friend.

Wadi laughed. 'We'll just hang out together and smoke.'

'Okay,' I told him. 'I'll be there in ten minutes.'

Mum was getting ready for work so I said I was meeting a friend.

'Which friend?' she asked.

'Vicky,' I lied.

Wadi was waiting for me when I arrived. I spotted him through the glass window of the shop. The closed sign was hanging in the front door so I wasn't sure what to do but Wadi signalled for me to go around the back.

'What kept you?' he laughed. I smiled up at him and noticed that he looked even older in strong daylight. When he smiled I spotted that some of his teeth were missing. For a split second I thought about turning back but then he said something.

'I'm having a cigarette, do you want one?'

I nodded – it was only a cigarette. I went into the back of the shop and stood against a bench. He lit up two cigs and handed one to me. I inhaled a mouthful and began to relax as the smoke filled my lungs.

'So, have you been smoking long?' Wadi asked.

I nodded and blew the rest of the smoke from my mouth.

'A few years,' I shrugged.

'Wow, and you're only fourteen?' he gasped.

I lowered my eyes to the ground. Wadi was staring at me intently and I didn't like it. Then he started to chuckle but I didn't know what he was laughing at. He took one last drag on his fag and crushed out the dying embers in an ashtray on a bench behind me. I wondered if he'd put the ashtray there on purpose because as soon as he'd done it he began to paw my body. I panicked because I didn't know what to do. I hated the feel of his hot hands but I wasn't sure if I was allowed to say no; he'd just given me a cigarette. He was always giving me things, and somehow it felt rude to say no after he'd been so kind and generous. My mind was still racing when Wadi clasped his hands around my waist and lifted me up onto the bench.

The bench was flimsy and even though I was slim, I was worried it'd give way. But Wadi didn't seem to care. He used it to sort out the day's newspapers and now he was using it to hold me there. Suddenly, I felt trapped with his legs straddled either side.

Without warning, he unzipped my pink hoodie. It was my

favourite. It had the word 'cheeky' written across the front. For a moment, I thought how cheeky it was of him to have done something like that without asking. As the zip slid down, my mind flashed back to Sam forcing me to have sex that day in the restaurant. My breathing became more laboured as I realised what was about to happen. But I was stuck, unable to move. Wadi had me anchored down on the bench. Maybe this was my fault? After all, I'd come here. What if people thought I'd led him on?

I wanted to push him away but he was stronger than me. Instead I shut my eyes and willed for it to be over. I was wearing a thin pink T-shirt but Wadi simply hooked his fingers underneath it and snaked his hands up inside. They felt rough and rubbed against my skin – it made my flesh crawl. I knew this was wrong – he was a grown man and I was a child, but I didn't know how to make it stop.

Then he let out a muffled moan as he curled up my top and pulled both breasts out of my bra, cupping them in his hands. Everything was happening too fast; I had no control. I'd come to the shop thinking we were going to share a cigarette…but now this. Wadi moaned as he sucked and licked at my breasts. His rubbery wet mouth felt disgusting against my body; he was disgusting. I opened my eyes and looked down. I saw the bald spot on the back of his head shine in the dim light. The more he worked his way across my body, the more his bulging belly pressed against my legs. I felt sick.

'You're lovely,' he gasped. My heart lurched as he moved a hand down inside my jeans. He snaked it down deep beneath my waistband and pulled at my knickers. Something inside my head snapped. I didn't want him touching me down there; it made me feel cheap, like a piece of meat.

'I think I'd better go,' I said, trying to climb down off the bench. But Wadi was having none of it. He ignored me and used all his strength to pin me back down.

'You're going nowhere,' he said. His face twisted in a way I'd never seen before – it scared me. 'You're not going anywhere because we're going to have sex.'

I tried to stifle my panic. Bile rose up inside my throat; I wanted to be sick. I gulped it back down. Anxiously, I glanced either side but his arms had me locked in. There was nothing I could do now, there was no escape.

'But there's no room,' I replied, saying something, anything, to get out of there.

'No, but there's plenty of room down here,' he said, pointing towards the floor.

'But I don't…I don't want to,' my eyes pleaded with him to let me go but he wasn't listening anymore.

Instead he dragged me off the bench and pushed me down onto the hard concrete floor. He lifted my arms above my head and pinned them down hard so it was impossible for me to escape. I shivered with both cold and fear as the damp from the floor seeped into my skin. I tried to move but the more I wriggled, the harder Wadi pushed down. His weight was crushing down on me, stealing the breath from my body.

With a yank of his hand, he undid my belt and pulled down my jeans, taking my knickers with them.

'*No!*' I screamed, panic rising in my voice. But it fell on deaf ears – he was in charge now.

Wadi allowed all his weight to rest against me, crushing my ribs. Using his free hand, he unzipped his own trousers and pulled them down.

'Now just lie there and be a good girl,' he sneered. His breath felt hot and disgusting against my face.

I'd never been this close to him before but now I could smell his body odour leaking out from underneath his armpits. I tried to scream but he put his free hand over my mouth. I closed my eyes because I knew it was pointless; no one could help me now. Wadi anchored me down and had sex with me.

The tears stung in my eyes. They dripped furiously down the side of my cheeks onto the floor. I knew then that there was no such thing as a free lunch, cigarettes, chocolate or bags of crisps. Now he was taking his payment – I was his payment.

Even though Wadi had sex with me against my will I didn't realise it was rape. It sounds crazy but I was young and naive. I didn't think he was breaking the law. I thought it was my fault, that I was somehow to blame for leading him on.

Afterwards I ran all the way home. Wadi's laughter was still ringing in my ears as I sprinted along the path. By the time I reached the end of the street I began to retch. The thought of what had just happened made me feel sick. I wanted to shout out and tell someone, but I blamed myself. I'd gone there even though I knew he fancied me. Perhaps this was all my doing, perhaps I'd led him on? I decided no one could know about this; I'd rather die than let that happen.

The following day, Mum noticed a bruise on the back my left arm where Wadi had gripped and pinned me down hard against the floor.

'I was fighting with Andrew,' I said, as quick as a flash.

Mum tutted and pulled a face. She'd believed me. I was safe, for now.

Days later, when Vicky asked me to go to the shop I couldn't think what to say. I didn't want to tell her what had happened but I knew that if I said no, she'd be suspicious. So I went. I was frightened when I saw him but Wadi was so utterly charming that I believed him and even forgave him when he started saying nice things to me again. It made me feel better about what had happened.

'You're so beautiful, Katie. You are my girlfriend and I love you,' he whispered when Vicky was out of earshot.

I liked it when he said those nice things. He told me I was his girlfriend and I thought that made it alright again. He'd had sex with me because I was his girlfriend. I wandered over to Vicky, who was glancing through a pile of magazines.

'Katie, look at the state of that,' she said, pointing to someone on the page but my mind was still elsewhere. Suddenly my mobile phone bleeped.

I glanced down at it: 'Let's meet again, xx'. It was a text from Wadi.

'Who is it?' asked Vicky, trying to read the screen.

'Just Lauren,' I replied, flipping the phone shut and throwing it back inside my school bag.

Vicky sighed and looked at the row of sweets.

'What shall we have tonight?' she said, running her fingers along the chocolate bars. But I didn't have an appetite. My stomach was too churned up for food.

I glanced over at Wadi. He winked and pointed down at his phone. I smiled weakly. I wasn't sure about this, or him, but maybe he was trying to be kind. He was my boyfriend – he'd told me so and now he just wanted to look after me. I was confused but part of me craved the love and attention he gave me.

After that I returned to the shop time and time again, without Vicky. I don't know why I went back, other than I loved the fact that Wadi seemed to worship me. Vicky didn't know Wadi and I were an item and I knew I wouldn't tell her. Wadi told me he loved me and I so desperately wanted to be loved. When he said I was special I believed him because I wanted to. Even having sex in the back of his shop became kind of normal after a while.

Sometimes, we'd go into the back, leaving Tali in charge behind the counter. It made me feel important, special even. But I often wondered if Tali knew what we were doing. I desperately hoped that he didn't think I was some cheap nasty little tart. But after a few months that's how I started to feel – I was a dirty girl and this was all I deserved. Bit by bit, I lost any respect I once had for myself.

'I'll look after you,' Wadi whispered in my ear.

His breath was hot against my neck. He was strong so I believed him when he said he'd protect me.

'I'd like that,' I replied numbly.

Wadi wasn't nasty or violent and he didn't call me names like the other boys at school. He was kind and generous as long as I kept him happy and had sex with him then everything would be alright. Only things weren't. I didn't realise it then but I was paying for his love and attention with my innocence.

A few weeks later I walked into the shop to find that Wadi wasn't there. Instead Tali stood up when he saw me walk through the door. We started to chat. It was obvious I liked Tali and soon he was flirting with me.

'Come upstairs, Katie,' he said, taking my hand.

I pulled it away playfully and looked up at him. Tali smiled and walked over to the door. He locked it and turned the red sign to 'closed'. I knew what was coming but I didn't mind. I liked Tali and he fancied me.

As we climbed the stairs at the back of the shop I felt a little giddy. I knew there was a flat above the shop because they were always carrying stock up there. But the flat was empty; no one lived there so we'd be all alone. Tali held my hand in his as he led me along a corridor, past a small bathroom and into a large bedroom. The room was empty apart from a double bed in the middle. The bed was unmade with only a stained mattress on top. I knew what he wanted, but unlike my first time with Wadi, I didn't feel frightened.

Tali kissed me, slowly at first. He told me how much he loved me – and I loved hearing him say those words. As he peeled away my clothes he kissed me and told me how special I was. His words meant more than Wadi's, because it was Tali that I really loved.

The surroundings were grim but it didn't matter because now I had two men who loved me and wanted to be with me. Before long I was having sex with both of them and even though they knew about one another, they didn't seem to mind sharing. Deep down, I knew it was wrong but I craved the love they gave me and somehow when they said they loved me it made it alright again. Even so, I didn't tell a soul. I didn't want the other girls to call me a slag; I shuddered at what they'd say if they knew. But the others were just silly little girls – they weren't grown-up, special and loved like me. I was loved by two men – Wadi and Tali were my boyfriends. I still saw Dean too but only very occasionally now. I preferred the others because they showered me with presents – cigarettes, alcohol, whatever I wanted. It didn't matter if the sex was sometimes rough, because they loved me.

'You're so pretty, Katie,' Tali told me time and time again. He flattered me constantly.

A few days after we'd had sex in the flat, Tali begged me to meet him again.

'I'll be in my car. I'll park behind the back of the shop – six o'clock.' He put a finger to his lips as if this was our secret. I grinned.

Later that night as I crept into the unlit alley I heard the familiar sound of a car engine. As I approached I saw the outline of a dark car – it was Tali, he was waiting just as he'd promised. My heart skipped a beat.

'Get in the back,' he whispered. I wasn't sure why he was whispering; maybe he didn't want Wadi to hear because it was obvious I loved Tali.

I fastened my seat belt and glanced sideways out of the car window. I expected Tali to drive away but instead we just sat there.

'No,' he hissed, with a downward wave of his hand, 'you need to lie down so that no one can see you.'

I stared at him blankly.

'I'm married,' he told me. 'I can't be seen driving through town with a white girl in the back of my car – people know me.'

I knew both Tali and Wadi had wives but it didn't bother me because I knew it was part of their culture to marry young. Sometimes I got a bit upset when I thought of Tali with his wife, but he assured me he'd never really loved her. He said she was ill and even though he wanted to leave, he couldn't because the shock would kill her.

Tali was still waiting for me to lie down on the back seat so I did as he said. After a quarter of an hour, we pulled into a petrol station on the outskirts of town. I knew where we were because I could see the neon sign lit up outside.

Tali turned to me.

'Katie, I need you to lie on the floor instead.'

I looked up at him, a bit confused.

'We can't risk you being seen,' he explained.

I nodded and climbed off the seat onto the floor below. It was cramped and the carpet felt rough and cheap against my face. I tried not to look too much. It was filthy down there with crumbs and mud off people's shoes. I heard Tali get out of the car and slam the door. Moments later he reappeared with something in his hand. He thrust a hand back down towards me on the floor and waved a packet in front of my face – it was a packet of condoms.

'You can't be too careful,' he winked.

I tried to smile back but my arms and legs had gone numb and the dust on the floor was making me sneeze.

'Shush!' Tali hissed. 'You'll get us caught!'

Lying down there, I felt every bump as we continued along the rest of our journey. Every pothole juddered through me as we rattled along the road. Soon we were in the countryside. I wasn't sure where but I knew I'd be safe with Tali. Suddenly he parked up the car and pulled on the handbrake.

'It's okay, you can sit up now,' he told me.

'Where are we?' I asked, peering out of the window. It was late and everything was black, and even though there was moonlight it was hard to make out shapes – I saw trees but not much else.

'We're in the country,' Tali grinned, 'where no one can find us.'

He undid his belt, walked around to the back of the car and climbed onto the back seat with me. We started to kiss. I was in the middle of nowhere with a grown man but I wasn't frightened. Tali would protect me, just as he promised.

He put his hand inside his jacket pocket and pulled out the box of condoms. The silver square wrapper glinted in the moonlight as he ripped it open. Tali pulled down my jeans and then we had sex.

'I love you,' he told me.

It meant everything to me to hear him say those words because I loved him too. I truly believed this was love. I wanted to stay right there in Tali's arms forever but then I noticed him glance down at his watch.

'I've got to go,' he announced.

Sadly, I sank back down onto the car floor so that he could drive us home. Half an hour later, we parked up in the same alleyway at the back of the shop and I hoisted myself back up onto the car seat.

'Hurry home,' he urged, as if I was a child. 'You don't want to be late.'

I felt a little hurt when he shooed me out of his car but I turned to give him one last wave. He waved back, started up the engine and roared off, leaving me standing there. I ran all the way home. When I reached the front door I was still smiling. I loved Tali and he loved me; everything was perfect. Soon we'd be together, just as he promised. I told myself that I'd finish things with Dean and Wadi and then we'd buy a house together, and I wouldn't have to live with Mum and Phil anymore; I'd be all grown up with a place of my own.

But Tali wanted me to grow up too quickly. The second time we had sex in the flat above the shop, he told me he wanted to try something different – he wanted to try anal sex, so we did. It hurt like hell and I got no enjoyment from it, but Tali said he loved me even more for letting him do it.

A few nights later, he picked me up in the usual place and

told me to lie down. But this time I refused because my back was hurting.

'I'll lie on the back seat but not on the floor,' I told him.

Tali rolled his eyes and muttered something under his breath. He was annoyed but I didn't want to lie on the smelly carpet anymore.

'Can't I sit up yet?' I begged, but he refused.

'We're not there yet!' he snapped.

I lifted my head up slightly to find out where we were but all I could see was trees. Thinking we were safe in the countryside, I sat up but when he saw me, Tali went mad.

'What are you doing?' he screamed. 'Get down!'

I shrugged my shoulders. There wasn't a soul around – he was panicking for nothing.

He was still trying to get me to lie down when we turned a corner. Suddenly we found ourselves surrounded by a group of women, all on horseback.

'Stay down, stay down,' Tali panicked, waving his left arm madly.

But I refused. I was sick of hiding – I loved Tali, we were going to be together soon, so what did it matter? I was proud that he was my boyfriend and I wanted everyone to see us.

After they'd passed, Tali screeched to a halt on a dirt track. He turned to face me – he was furious.

'You're going to get me caught!' he shouted.

'So what?' I answered back. 'Then you'll have to leave your wife and kids, and then we'll be together.'

But he wasn't listening: he was furious I'd disobeyed him.

A week later, I caught him looking at his mobile phone.

'Here, let me take a picture?' he suggested.

I was naked, lying on top of the bed in the flat above the shop.

'No, I've got no clothes on!' I giggled, trying to cover myself up.

'It doesn't matter, you don't need clothes. You're beautiful as you are.'

I smiled and lay back down. Tali had just called me beautiful and I felt it. He took dozens of pictures of me. I giggled because I knew it was naughty.

'This will give me something to look at when I'm not with you,' he grinned.

I kissed him. I didn't mind – I was glad that Tali wanted to see me naked because it made me feel sexy.

A few weeks later, he was flicking through his phone when I spotted something – the photographs he'd taken of me, only this time they made me feel uncomfortable.

'Delete them, please!' I begged.

Tali pulled a sad face. 'Okay, Katie, anything for you.'

But he didn't delete the photographs. Instead he persuaded me to let him take even more.

'I'm not sure,' I told him.

I don't know what had changed but something had. Tali loved me but suddenly him taking naked photos of me on his phone made me feel dirty.

'But I love you,' Tali insisted. 'I'm going to buy you a house and we'll move in together as soon as I can.'

'But why can't we live together now?' I asked.

'It's my wife, Katie – you know she's sick.'

I pushed his arms away.

'Just leave her,' I demanded, 'then we can be together, forever.'

Tali shook his head. 'Not while she's sick, it wouldn't be right. I will leave her but I can't yet.'

I wanted Tali to be with me, not his wife, and I knew he did too. Then it dawned on me: I was sleeping with Wadi on the nights I wasn't with Tali, and then there was Dean. In many ways, I had three men fighting for my attention. I never told him but I cringed every time Wadi came near me. His bulging belly and badly-dyed hair repulsed me and the bald spot at the back of his head seemed to get wider each month. It was a sign of age but it revolted me because I was still so young.

I thought if I slept with Wadi then Tali might get jealous, leave his wife and live with me. But then if this was love, why did we have to hide away and have sex in secret on the back seat of a car or on a dirty mattress above a shop?

When I was with Wadi, we had sex on the floor just as I'd done with Sam. Only now it was in the back of a shop and not a restaurant. As far as I knew Sam didn't know the others but it seemed they all wanted me. I wondered if, perhaps, Asian men were attracted to me for some reason – maybe I was special.

Even though I didn't recognise it then, my life was in freefall. But things were about to get much worse, for soon I was going to meet the Devil himself.

CHAPTER 12

A MONSTER CALLED ZEB

My mobile buzzed on top of the dressing table. I presumed it was Dean, Wadi or Tali calling but when I glanced down I saw another number – one I didn't recognise.

'Hello?' I answered, my voice so low it was barely a whisper. Whoever it was, I didn't want Mum to hear.

'Is that Katie?' a man's voice asked. I didn't recognise it.

'Yes, who is this?' I was confused; I didn't recognise either the voice or the number.

'That doesn't matter,' the man laughed. I was annoyed. It was a reasonable thing to ask – he'd called me.

'It does,' I replied.

'No, it doesn't. Listen, Katie, I want to meet you,' the man said.

An alarm bell rang inside my head. I didn't know this man yet he seemed to know me.

'Sam?' I guessed, even though I knew it wasn't Sam's voice.

'No, it's not Sam, but like I say, that doesn't matter. Hey, do you like going to the movies?' he asked, suddenly changing the subject.

I loved going to the pictures but I wanted to know who this cheeky man was.

'Depends who's asking,' I said, trying to catch him out. But he wouldn't tell me.

'Me, I'm asking. Now, you haven't answered my question, do you want to go to the cinema, maybe have a bite to eat before?'

It was a tempting offer. I never went out for meals unless it was a birthday or a special occasion. It was the same for the cinema too.

I thought of Wadi. He'd been kind, but he'd never offered to take me to the cinema or for a meal. Maybe that's what was wrong with our relationship. This stranger, whoever he was, sounded much nicer than him, offering to take me places.

'Err…how did you get my number?' I asked, as soon as the thought occurred to me.

'That doesn't matter.'

'Just like your name,' I quipped.

The voice laughed and this time I laughed along too.

'Yeah, something like that. Now when are you going to let me take you out?'

'I'll think about it,' I replied and with that, I hung up.

I thought the man, whoever he was, would give up but the fact that I played hard to get made him call me more.

The following day, my mobile rang again. It was him.

'When am I taking you out, then?'

His sheer gall made me laugh and the more he flirted with me, the more I flirted back.

'I said I'll think about it,' I giggled.

'Well, don't take too long!'

After that the calls and texts increased until I felt under pressure to meet up with this stranger.

'Come on, I just want to chill out. Do you like chilling out?' he said.

'Yeah…'

'Well, we can chill out together then.'

I liked the attention this perfect stranger was paying me. I didn't stop to think why he'd be asking me out.

At first I presumed he knew Sam, Wadi or Tali, but he said he didn't. I was baffled. But still he persisted and called every day until finally I felt as if I knew him.

'I like you,' the voice admitted, 'and I want to get to know you better.'

In the end, after a couple of weeks, I relented.

'Okay, okay,' I sighed. 'I'll meet you. Where?'

The man suggested the same parade where Wadi's shop was.

'Do you know the shop on the corner?' he asked.

Of course, I knew it well – it was where I met Wadi and Tali.

'Great, I'll meet you at the back of there tomorrow, about 5pm. We'll go out, to the cinema and then for a bite to eat.'

I was excited. The man sounded really nice – I was looking forward to being spoilt for a change. He noted the excitement in my voice, and suddenly his tone changed.

'Don't wait at the front, meet me at the back. I'll be in a car,' he insisted.

My heart lurched at the word 'car'. I tried to shake off the awful feeling from the back of my mind but I couldn't. He was a stranger after all.

'Maybe this isn't such a good idea…' I said.

'Nonsense, I'll see you then. I'm looking forward to meeting you, Katie, and chilling out with you. Now don't be late and don't forget,' he told me.

He was very persuasive and forceful; he made me feel like he was in charge and now I felt too scared to back out.

The following night after school I pulled on a pair of jeans and my pink hoodie top and some trainers. I told Mum I was going to Vicky's so she wouldn't worry but she was off to work so I knew she wouldn't know how long I'd been gone. I walked to the back of the shop but as I approached, I spotted two people sat inside. Maybe I'd got the wrong car? I was just about to turn and walk away when a familiar voice called.

'Katie, over here.'

And that's when I saw him – my mystery caller. He was Asian and much better-looking than I thought he would be. He was younger than Tali and Wadi but older than Sam. He was a man, not a teenager. I guessed he was in his early twenties.

Apprehensively I walked towards him but as I did, he began to smile.

'I didn't think you were coming!' he laughed, trying to lift the tense atmosphere. My eyes darted from him to the other man, who was sitting in the driver's seat.

'I...I...I thought you'd be alone,' I stammered.

'Oh, him,' he said, pointing at the other man. 'This is my friend Aban. He's driving so I can have a drink, with you.'

It made sense. But when he asked me to get in the back of the car something made me hesitate.

'What's the matter, Katie?' he said, his voice mocking me as if I was a silly little girl. 'I'm not going to hurt you. I told you, I'm taking you out. You're a pretty girl and I want to chill with you.'

I thought about the meal he'd promised, the trip to the cinema. I'd come here tonight and I didn't want to back out now. Not only would I look stupid, I'd miss out on the treat too.

'Okay,' I agreed and with that, I climbed into the back of the car.

Aban put on some loud music and I noticed they were smoking something.

'Want a drag?' the man asked.

'I don't know your name,' I said. Even though I'd asked countless times, he'd still not told me.

'It's Zebadiyah,' he replied, taking another drag on the cigarette. He blew the smoke in my face and smiled. It smelt sweet. I looked at the roll-up in his hand – it was dope.

'Zeba-di-yah,' I said slowly, trying to repeat it but it made him laugh. I felt young and foolish.

'Just call me Zeb, that's what my friends call me for short.'

'Zeb?' I replied.

'Uh huh,' said Zeb, passing me the joint. 'You want some? It'll relax you.'

I took it from his fingers and slowly inhaled the sweet dope. As soon as I did so I felt my body relax and melt into the seat of the car: this was strong dope.

'Better?' asked Zeb.

'Yeah,' I sighed, trying to stay cool. I allowed my head to roll back against the headrest.

Aban started up the car engine and we drove off. I glanced out at the dreary town. Familiar sights passed by in a blur as we whizzed along. We drove past my school and up towards the main town; we passed shops, take-away restaurants, a large pub, supermarket and garage. Finally, the town gave way to fields as we accelerated along a dual carriageway, far away from the town centre. As the car gathered speed I watched as the familiar landmarks disappeared behind us. Then it hit me – I didn't have a clue where we were going.

'Where are you taking me?' I asked, beginning to panic.

The dope had numbed me for a while but now I was back with it – my senses were on full alert. I sat bolt upright and anxiously looked out the car window for something I recognised. But we were out of town and I didn't know where we were.

'Don't worry, Katie,' Zeb replied. 'We're going to chill, that's all.'

He leaned forward and turned up the music.

His friend shot him a glance – Aban looked anxious, which made me feel even worse. By now my heart was pumping on adrenalin.

'But I thought we were going to the cinema…' I said, the words sounding ridiculous as I said them.

Zeb took a long drag on the spliff.

'Relax. Chill, Katie, I'm going to look after you. We can go to the pictures anytime.'

My throat constricted with fear. I tried to gulp but my mouth felt bone dry. As the fear rose, my stomach knotted and twisted with anxiety.

Oh my God, I thought, *they're going to kill me!*

My mind raced with every possible scenario. What if they killed me and dumped my body in a field? What if they strangled me? Maybe they had a knife, or even a gun? Why had I been so stupid? I was only fourteen years old – why had I climbed into a car with two strange men? How could I have been so stupid?

I thought of Mum waiting back home for me and furtively glanced down at my handbag. My mobile phone was inside – I knew exactly where it was. If I was careful I'd be able to sneak it out and call someone. But how would I speak without them hearing? Also, my bag was zipped, so I'd have to undo it first – they might notice and hurt me more. I was too terrified to try anything, so instead I remained frozen to the spot. I looked out of the window and prayed they wouldn't kill me.

I pictured Mum looking at her watch, wondering where on earth I was. I imagined my body buried somewhere remote – abandoned, where no one would ever find me. I'd be dead in a field or a wood and no one would ever see me again.

I cursed myself. What the hell had I been thinking? I knew I needed to do or say something to survive.

'Where are you taking me?' I demanded.

I tried to sound confident – I didn't want these men to sense my fear. If I sounded strong enough, then perhaps they'd let me go. But they didn't answer.

After ten minutes of dual carriageways and fields, we turned left off a roundabout and headed into another small town. I felt reassured by the presence of other people, buildings and houses. My eyes searched for a road sign – I needed to know where I was. I recognised the town. It was the next one along from mine but not one I knew very well at all.

As we passed by more streets and houses, I slowly began to feel better. I'd let my imagination run away with me. Maybe there was a cafe or a restaurant here they were taking me to.

'Is it far?' I asked hopefully, waiting for them to tell me where we were going. But neither man replied.

Without warning, we turned into a narrow street. It was

lined with terraced houses. The car slowed down, the click of the indicator signalled and we parked up. But there was no restaurant here, just houses.

'Where are we?' I asked again.

Zeb twisted the windscreen mirror between his fingers so he could see my reflection.

'You'll see.' He grinned.

His words, the look on his face and the way he spoke unnerved me. I didn't want to be here with two strange men on my own. I was fourteen years old – I wanted to be safe with Mum and Phil.

Zeb unfastened his seatbelt and opened the car door at the side of him.

'Where are you going?' I asked, my voice full of fear. By now I couldn't hide it.

I looked out of the window and saw a small terraced house with a plain white plastic door. It looked like every other one in the street.

'What are we doing here?' I said.

Zeb turned to me in his seat. He had one foot on the wet pavement outside and one foot still inside the car.

'I'm going to get out of the car and go to that door,' he said, pointing over to the white uPVC door of the house. 'I'm going to unlock it and I want you to wait a few minutes and then follow me inside.'

'But I thought we were going to the cinema? That's what you said…' My voice cracked and I realised just how small and frightened I really was.

'I said we're going to chill and we are,' he said, pointing back at the house. 'We're going to chill in there.'

'But I don't want to…' I protested.

Zeb raised his hand in mid-air to shut me up.

'Listen, stop being paranoid! Nothing's going to happen. We're going to chill, okay. Just do as I say.'

With that he turned and climbed out of the car. The door slammed. I tried to look at Aban but he wouldn't look at me; instead, he stared straight ahead. I could tell he didn't want to be there either. I realised in that moment that Zeb had some kind of hold over him. Aban was his friend, yet he was frightened of Zeb.

I opened the car window slightly to get some air. I could hear Zeb's footsteps on the wet pavement as he strolled to the front door. He double-checked, looking up and down the street, and pulled something from his pocket – a bunch of keys. They jangled slightly as he separated one from the rest and slid it into the lock. The key twisted to the side and the door swung open. But it was dark and I couldn't see properly. Zeb stepped inside and shut the front door. Moments later a light flicked on in the downstairs room and then I spotted him at the front window, drawing a heavy curtain across.

I gulped. I wondered why he didn't want anyone to see in – what was he planning to do to me? My mind raced. Then something occurred to me – what if he wasn't alone? What if there were others waiting to pounce?

I cursed myself a second time. How had I got into this mess and how could I have been so stupid?

Adrenalin and fear pumped so fast through my veins that I could hear the blood gushing inside my brain. My body was in panic mode. I was so agitated that I almost didn't hear Aban when he spoke to me.

'You need to go in now,' he insisted.

But I didn't want to go in; I didn't want to move an inch. I didn't want to get out of the car or leave Aban because even though I didn't really know him, I knew I felt safer with him than with Zeb.

'But I don't want to,' I said, my voice desperate. I pleaded with Aban not to make me but he wouldn't listen.

'He's waiting inside for you and you don't want to keep him waiting…' he said, his voice trailing off.

Aban didn't have to finish his sentence. Zeb was trouble – it was obvious. He was a dangerous man. He'd been pushy and he'd pressurised me over the phone until I'd agreed to meet him. He always got what he wanted, you could just tell.

My hands were shaking as I unfastened my seatbelt and pulled open the car door. My heart was in my mouth as I turned towards the house. I was only a teenager and I knew I was way out of my depth. Zeb was a grown man – a complete stranger.

Taking another deep breath I slowly walked towards the door. I didn't know if I was supposed to knock or not; Zeb hadn't told me. My heart was pounding and every sinew of my body told me to turn and run away. But I couldn't – I was simply terrified. I couldn't outrun a car; I didn't know a soul here in this other town. There was no way out, it was too late.

The door swung open and I saw Zeb standing there. With a dramatic sweep of his hand he invited me in.

'What took you so long? I've been waiting,' he grinned.

The light in the front room shone against his face and for the first time I realised he was a little younger than I'd first thought, but he was still a man.

The door clicked behind me – I felt trapped. I was with a strange man in a strange house and I didn't know what to do or how to get home.

I'll just have to do everything he tells me, I thought. *It's the only way I'll get home safe.*

It seemed alien to think so straight at a time like this but I knew I needed a plan if I wanted to get out of there.

My eyes scanned the room; it was sparse and unloved with very little furniture inside. The front room was open-plan with a living area at the front and a kitchen at the back. But then I noticed something else; there was no cooker, only a sink and taps. I thought it odd – a kitchen without a cooker. There was a door to my left but I didn't know what was behind it because it was closed. The living room was empty apart from a TV, coffee table and two sofas. I turned to face Zeb.

'So, what are we doing here?' I asked. My forced confidence masked the sheer terror I felt inside.

'Come,' he said, taking me by the hand. 'I want to talk to you…but not down here. I want to talk to you upstairs.'

He pushed down the handle of the closed door and pulled it open. I peered through and saw a set of stairs. Zeb pulled at my hand but I hesitated and tried to let go.

'What?' he asked, a little more gently. 'I just want to talk to you, that's all.'

I was frightened but I was too scared to refuse, terrified of what he'd do to me if I said no.

'Okay,' I agreed weakly and we began to climb the stairs.

We walked up the first set of stairs onto a landing and that's when I noticed a bedroom leading off it.

'No, not in there. We're going to the room at the top.'

I gulped. I didn't want to go to the room at the top – I wanted to turn and run the other way, down the stairs and out onto the street outside. But Aban was there and he'd stop me.

There was another door at the end of the corridor which led

to a bathroom. Everything looked normal so far and, thankfully, we seemed to be alone. I breathed a sigh of relief. As we passed the bathroom I noticed how filthy it was. There was scum around the sink. I knew this wasn't a normal house – it looked like a doss house.

We arrived at the top of the second set of stairs and Zeb turned sharply to his left. We'd reached the room on the top floor.

The room was dark inside so Zeb ran his hand along the wall and clicked on the light switch. The walls were a filthy, discoloured blue. It was a scruffy, empty room apart from an unmade king-size bed in the middle with a sofa situated opposite in a corner of the room. My heart sank as Zeb walked over to the bed. It had no sheets, only a stained mattress. For a minute I thought he was going to make me lie down on it with him but instead he flung his coat down on top of it.

'Come,' he said, walking over to the sofa and flopping down upon it. His hand patted the empty space beside him.

'Come and sit with me.'

I was too frightened to say no so I sat down. I sat and waited for him to pounce but instead he started to talk.

'I want to be with you,' he said, 'but I can't. You can't ever be my girlfriend because I live with my mum and dad and you are white. They would never accept a white girl in their home.'

I began to relax. Maybe he liked me but couldn't be seen with me, just like Sam and Tali. That's why he'd brought me here. Maybe this was just like Sam's restaurant?

'I like you, Katie,' said Zeb, pulling a spliff from his pocket. He lit it and took a drag.

'Want some?' he asked.

'Yeah,' I said. Nervous relief washed over me and for the first time, I felt better. He'd said we'd chill and now we were. We'd probably just smoke the joint and leave.

Zeb handed the spliff to me.

'I can't be with you, Katie, I can't be your boyfriend,' he explained again. But he didn't have to; I knew how it worked and I didn't mind. I wasn't looking for a new boyfriend anyway – I already had three.

'What do you do?' I asked, changing the subject. 'Do you work?'

Zeb shook his head.

'No, no, I'm at college,' he replied. 'I want to learn so I can get a good job.'

I was just about to ask what he was studying when Zeb leaned forward and kissed me. It was sudden and unexpected and I wasn't sure quite what to do. But the spliff relaxed me and all the fear I'd felt disappeared. Maybe Zeb wasn't so bad after all?

Just as I began to trust him, Zeb undid the zip on his jeans.

'I want you to give me a blow job,' he insisted, his voice harsh and cold.

'No,' I refused.

'Listen, Katie, I want a blow job and you are going to give me one, whether you like it or not.'

I looked around me. I thought about making a run for it but the door was at the other side of the room. It was hopeless – Zeb would catch me. He might lose his temper and push me down the stairs. The room was airless; there wasn't even a window at the front, only a skylight. No one apart from Zeb and Aban knew I was there; I was trapped. I thought back to my original plan. If I gave him what he wanted then that would be it – he'd let me go home.

'Give me a blow job, now,' he said, roughly grabbing the back of my head.

I cried with pain as he tugged and twisted my long hair between his fingers. He forced my face into his crotch. I was shaking with fear. In an instant Zeb had changed from Mr Nice Guy to something else entirely.

'Listen, I don't give a fuck if you don't want to do it, you're going to do it anyway,' he screamed at me. He grabbed my face, pulled down his pants and forced my head onto him. I shut my eyes and tried to shut off my mind as I did as he asked. He was in control now, not me.

At one point, I tried to pull away but he was stronger and he forced me back down. It was no good. *The sooner I did as he asked*, I thought, *the sooner I could leave*. But then the plan changed again.

'Take off your clothes!' he barked.

I trembled on the sofa and wrapped my arms protectively across my chest.

'But I don't want to…'

'I don't give a fuck what you want, take them off now! Take them *all* off!' he screamed.

His eyes were wild and his faced crazed with anger. I was terrified what he'd do if I didn't obey.

'Take them off now!' he shouted again. This time his voice and body rose with anger and he turned to face me square on. I cowered beneath him.

'If you don't take them off, I'll fucking rip them off, understand?'

I nodded weakly and began to take off my clothes. I'd been naked with Sam, Tali, Wadi and Dean but that was different, they were my boyfriends – Zeb was a stranger. I didn't know what he was capable of.

'You're going to do this,' he said as he forced me to lie on the sofa.

I watched as he pulled something from his trouser pocket. It was a condom.

He lay down on top of me, the dead weight of his body pinning me down. The cheap fabric of the sofa rubbed against my back and legs as he raped me.

I tried to get up, to push him off but it was no good. He was so much stronger – I didn't stand a chance.

At one point I screamed out loud but it just made him worse.

'What the fuck are you doing?' he said, clamping a hand across my mouth. Suddenly I couldn't breathe. I thought I'd black out but I managed to wriggle from underneath his hand and snort through my nostrils. I sounded like a frightened animal – he was treating me like an animal.

'I said keep the fuck down!' he hollered, giving me another hard shove. He knelt on the top of my arms so I couldn't move.

I looked up and saw the bare light bulb and the filthy flaked painted ceiling. I tried to separate my mind from what was happening but it was no good. I was here and I was being raped by a complete stranger. I wanted to die – death would be better than this.

Afterwards, Zeb pulled his boxer shorts and jeans back up. He'd kept his top on throughout. I wondered why and then I realised it was so I couldn't scratch his body.

'Get up,' he hissed but I couldn't move. I was shivering. Naked, I curled up into a ball – the foetal position – but my eyes remained wide with fear because I didn't know what he'd do next.

'Get up and get dressed,' he said, picking up my bundle of

clothes from the floor. He bunched them up in his hands and threw them at me like rags.

'Get dressed and come downstairs.'

Frozen with fear, I watched as he walked towards the door and slammed it behind him. I heard his footsteps on the stairs and let out a sigh of relief. It was over, for now. I looked down at my body. Had that really just happened?

My hands were trembling as I pulled up my knickers and dragged on my jeans. It made me feel a little better, covering up my body. It felt good, like a cloth armour. It wouldn't protect me from Zeb but I had to cover myself – he'd seen enough of me.

I had been raped. The words stuck inside my head. *I'd been raped by a stranger*. But I'd agreed to come here, so it was my fault. I'd come to this deserted house in a different part of town. I'd allowed Zeb to bring me up here to this room and let him kiss me. My whole body shuddered with revulsion as I thought of it and what had followed.

People would call me an idiot for trusting a complete stranger. They'd say it was all my fault and I'd got what I deserved. Maybe those girls at school had been right about me, maybe I was stupid.

I was still blaming myself when I heard a voice; it was Zeb calling up to me.

'Katie, are you ready? I'm waiting for you.'

CHAPTER 13

THE SECRET HOUSE

'**D**on't tell anyone you've been here,' Zeb hissed as soon as I stepped into the living room. I'd just been raped and I couldn't stop shaking.

'No one must ever know about this house, understand?' His voice was harsh and his eyes cold.

'Yes,' I nodded, my voice barely a whisper. I was so frightened; I couldn't even look at him.

My body was numb with shock. I'd been raped right here in this house whilst families busied themselves just feet away, on the other side of the wall.

Zeb was sat on the sofa smoking another spliff. The TV was blaring away to itself in a corner of the room. He was facing it but I could tell he wasn't watching.

I found a place on the other sofa next to Aban. He must have come into the house when I was upstairs. I tried to look up at him. Did he know what Zeb had just done? Had he heard us upstairs? Was he in on the whole thing? I tried to catch his eye but he continued to stare straight ahead.

Zeb was trying to talk to me. He was acting nice in front of Aban, as though the last half an hour hadn't happened.

'Are you alright, Katie?' he asked.

I flinched as I watched him cross the room. He told Aban to budge up and make some room. Zeb nestled himself down on the sofa beside me and I felt my skin crawl at the touch of his hand against my face.

I wanted to shout it out: *You've just raped me, why would I be alright?* But I was terrified. Anxiety tightened inside me like a balled fist. I was too frightened to reply – too scared to speak in case I said the wrong thing and angered him more. Instead I sat in a numbed silence.

'Okay?' he asked again. I tried not to look at him but his hand moved from my face to my hair. He stroked it and I flinched once more. This time he noticed.

'You have to go home now,' he said suddenly, rising to his feet.

Aban got up too. He grabbed the remote control and flicked off the TV. He was in on this, he had to be. He'd not raped me but he'd played his part – he'd driven me here to the secret house. He'd allowed this monster to bring me here and rape me. How could he not know?

Aban opened the door and waited for me to follow. I turned to see Zeb. He sat back down and lit another spliff. I breathed a sigh of relief – it was obvious he wasn't coming with us.

As I turned to leave, Zeb called me and I automatically froze.

'My friend will take you but I'll call you again soon, okay?'

But I knew it wasn't a question: I had no choice because I was terrified of him. If Zeb wanted to see me again, he would. He'd make the decisions. I felt powerless against him. I thought about telling someone, but who would I tell and what would I say? That I got into a car with two strange men and let them drive me miles away to a strange house in a strange town? They would say I deserved it and maybe they'd be right – maybe this was all I deserved now.

Aban drove me home in complete silence. I didn't doubt for one minute that he would try anything on with me. He did what Zeb told him and Zeb made it clear I was his property, no one else's.

As the car pulled up at the back of the newsagents, I didn't say a word. Instead I opened up the door and stepped out into the darkened alleyway. I hadn't even fastened my seatbelt on the journey home – what was the point? I'd already been hurt in the most unimaginable way. The thought of lying dead in the road brought me a perverse kind of comfort. At that moment, death seemed preferable to how I felt right now. At least if I was dead I wouldn't remember every sickening second – his breath on my face, his body on mine, the ripping agony as he forced himself inside me.

I waited until I saw the red lights of Aban's car turn right and disappear off onto the main road. I waited because I didn't want him to follow me home and see where I lived. Finally, when I was sure he was gone, I ran. As my feet picked up speed my mind replayed every moment over and over again like a sick film trailer.

The smell of Mum's cooking hit me as soon as I opened the front door. It turned my stomach.

'Is that you?' she called from the kitchen.

'Yeah,' I replied. Even my voice sounded different. It was tense and broken as though I'd become a different person in just one night.

'Your tea has been ready for ages,' Mum moaned as I walked past her in the hallway and headed up the stairs.

'I'm not hungry,' I mumbled. It was true – I felt sick.

'But where have you been? You should've been home ages ago.'

She was still scolding me as I reached the top of the stairs. But I didn't want to talk or to answer any of Mum's difficult questions; I just wanted to be alone.

'Sorry,' I called back down.

I saw the bathroom in front of me. I walked in and locked the door.

Mum's voice was slightly muffled downstairs but I could hear her talking to Phil.

'I don't know what's got into her these days. Maybe it's hormones – I don't know,' she huffed.

'She's just a kid, she'll snap out of it,' I heard Phil say.

But they didn't have a clue. They didn't know I'd just been attacked by a strange man in a secret house that I wasn't allowed to tell anyone about. For a split second I thought about ripping open the bathroom door and screaming, *I'll tell you what's wrong, I've just been raped!*

Although the thought was in my head I didn't know where to even begin or how to tell them. I knew there'd be too many questions – ones I didn't want to answer. They'd want to know where Zeb had got my number from but I didn't know. Only Sam, Wadi and Tali had my mobile number – had one of them given it to Zeb?

I knew Mum would go crackers at me for going off with

strangers. *What have I always told you about going off with people you don't know?* she'd say.

I could hear her now. If she knew about Zeb, then I'd have to tell her about Sam, Wadi and Tali – I'd be in so much trouble. She'd find out I'd been having sex with different men. I shuddered when I thought of it. Phil would find out and then there was Dad – they'd be sure to tell him. They might even call the police and then I'd be in loads of trouble because I was only fourteen. The whole school would find out and my life wouldn't be worth living. They'd all call me a slag.

No, I decided, this was one secret I'd keep to myself.

Instead I clicked on the shower and allowed my clothes to fall onto the floor around my feet. As the water washed over my face and streamed down my body I took out the flannel and began to scrub. I had to get his scent off me – I had to remove every trace of him from my skin. The bubbles foamed and frothed on the pink washcloth as I scrubbed and scrubbed, trying to get clean once more. I turned the thermostat control as high as I could bear. The water scalded my skin. It was so hot it felt as though the heat would strip it right off down to the bone, but I needed to be rid of him and his germs.

Eventually, I patted myself dry and wrapped the towel around my body. I glanced down at my clothes – they'd still be contaminated. I balled them up in my hands and pushed them deep down into the wash basket. I didn't care if I never saw them again because they would always remind me of what had happened that night.

I padded along the hallway to my bedroom and closed the door. I sat on the bed and looked around the room and then I saw it on the floor, next to the radiator: my pencil case. I grabbed it and pulled the zip open. My eyes scanned inside but I didn't have to look too hard – the sharpener was right there.

Undoing the screw, I pulled out the blade. I knew what needed to be done and I wasn't frightened – not anymore. I felt glad, glad that I had something to take away the pain. The steel blade cut into my soft skin like a knife against butter. I sighed with relief as a crimson stripe immediately appeared and blood began to flow down my wrist. The cut had been deep, but deep was good. Deep meant more blood and more relief. It was as though my blood contained all the badness inside. Now it was spilling out, and the badness was coming out with it.

I slashed again and again until my right arm was so shredded it looked as though I'd pushed it through a glass window. Soon the blood covered the uncut skin until I couldn't see pink flesh anymore. The cuts were so deep that blood began to drip down onto the duvet.

'Shit!' I cursed. I grabbed a box of tissues and tried to stem the flow.

I knew I'd gone too far. It took ages to stop bleeding but eventually it subsided and my wounds began to crust over.

I fell into a fitful night's sleep where I was plagued by monsters, murderers and rapists all trying to hurt me. The face on each one was always the same – it was the face of Zeb. In my dream I tried to run away from him but something would prevent me from escaping. My feet became tangled in imaginary weeds or I would trip up and fall at the wrong moment. Zeb always caught me in the end.

The following day I was exhausted through lack of sleep. Bleary-eyed I pulled down the sleeves of my school jumper so that Mum wouldn't see what I'd done to my arm. But then I realised – I'd need more than a jumper because later that afternoon I had PE lesson.

Phil was in the bathroom, having a shower. As soon as I heard him leave, I ran into the bathroom and shut the door. I opened up the cabinet and rummaged around with my hand until I found a pack of plasters. They were old and wedged at the back but it didn't matter, they'd have to do.

Later that day before the lesson, I slipped into the toilet and looked in the packet for the longest plaster I could find. It looked dramatic and ridiculous on my arm but it would do the job. I came out of the cubicle and walked over to the changing rooms where the rest of the class was getting changed.

'What have you done to your arm?' Megan immediately asked as soon as I took off my jumper.

I felt my face flush.

'I fell into a rose bush on the way home from school – I wasn't looking where I was going. It was dead funny,' I lied, a false grin spreading across my face.

Megan eyed the plaster and looked back at me. Her face was so concerned it made me want to weep.

'It looks really sore,' she said.

'Oh, it's okay. I've just made a bit of a mess of it, that's all.'

I changed the subject and we chatted about the lesson ahead. I didn't know if she believed me about the cuts and part of me worried that she'd tell Lauren.

After that, I decided I needed to be more careful. From now on I'd have to keep my scars and plasters hidden.

One morning, I was running late for school. I pulled on my dressing gown and made my way downstairs to the kitchen. I was so tired that I didn't notice when my right sleeve slipped down as I reached up to the cupboard for a glass.

'What's that on your arm?' Andrew gasped. He was standing by the sink but had turned in time to see.

At first I didn't have a clue what he was talking about. My mind was still fuggy with sleep but then I remembered the cuts.

'Nothing,' I snapped defensively. I grabbed at the cuff of my dressing gown but he pulled it back to get a better look.

'What have you done to your arm?' he shrieked.

I refused to answer.

'Well,' he threatened, 'let's see what Mum has to say about it.'

'It's none of your business!' I snapped but he wasn't listening. Now he'd seen I knew he'd tell Mum.

I slipped out for school without another word. All day long I dreaded going back home because I knew she'd be waiting for me, waiting for answers I didn't have.

'Let me see your arms,' Mum ordered as soon as I walked in.

My heart froze.

'It's nothing,' I pleaded. 'Whatever he's told you…he's lying.'

'Arms, NOW!' she shouted, grabbing my right arm.

Mum pulled up the sleeve of my school jumper and her face physically winced when she saw the cuts.

'Why, Katie? Why have you done that to yourself?'

But I couldn't tell her because I didn't know myself. I only knew I liked cutting myself because it made me feel better – it stopped the pain.

I thought about Zeb and the rape. Sam, Wadi and Tali – all the dirty sex I'd been having with different men. Mum looked at me.

'Why?' she demanded to know.

I didn't know what to say so I just shrugged. Mum was dumbstruck and didn't know what to do.

'Well,' she said. 'Whatever it is, it's stupid and I want you to stop it right now.'

'Okay,' I mumbled.

'Do you understand?' she insisted. She looked at me but I couldn't face her. I didn't want her to see there was more I was keeping from her.

'Okay,' I agreed, pulling back my arm.

'Why do you always have to be such a drama queen?' Mum asked.

I wanted to tell her, but what could I say? This wasn't attention-seeking – this was self-harm. I was doing it because I hated my life. I hated Zeb and what he'd done to me. I hated the bullies at school and how crap they made me feel. Maybe, in the back of my mind, I was subconsciously harming myself to draw attention so that someone, *anyone*, would ask me what was making me feel so bad. Maybe it was a cry for help; maybe I wanted someone to ask. But, other than Megan, no one ever did.

I grabbed my school bag off the floor. Mum rolled her eyes in annoyance as I pushed past her and went upstairs to my bedroom. Half an hour later the blade was back in my hand as I made a fresh cut.

That night I lay on my bed and thought about what Zeb had said. He'd told me not to tell. I wanted to, but I was frightened of him and what he'd do to me if I did.

And then there was Dean. We'd still been seeing each other but my time was now taken up with all these other men and there was very little space left for him. Now all I did was make excuses why we couldn't meet. Even when we managed to get together, my mobile phone would bleep with text messages. I told him it was Lauren but I knew he didn't believe me. He was sick of it and looked at me as though he didn't even know who I was anymore. I hardly knew myself.

The following day, I was so lost in my thoughts that at first I didn't see a girl in the year above walking in front of me along the pavement. But she kept turning round and that's when I noticed her. She turned again and whispered something to her friend. The other girl shot me a nasty look and the two of them smirked and laughed. I looked behind but there was no one there. They were laughing at me. I knew I should cross the road but when I did, the girls followed.

Fear rose inside me and the palms of my hands began to sweat. I knew what this meant. I turned and began to walk in the opposite direction but as I did, the first girl followed. 'Hey, Dumbo!' she called.

I started to run but the girl ran after me. My feet were moving as fast as they could but my school bag was heavy and it kept slipping off my shoulder, slowing me up.

I felt a shove between my shoulders – the force knocked me off my feet and I landed in a crumpled heap on the ground. I was on my side, winded and unsure what to do. The girl was standing over me and, with one swift movement, kicked me in the back and then began to kick me again and again. An excruciating pain seared up my spine. Humiliation flooded through me as a large group gathered to watch her kicking me like a dog on the ground.

When I finally looked up my heart sank – I spotted my friends standing there. But no one came to my aid, they were too frightened. Instead I took my beating.

Suddenly a man stepped in between us. He'd heard the commotion and came running over.

'Are you okay?' he asked, helping me to my feet.

He looked at the girl but she ran off.

'I just want to go home,' I began to sob.

The others saw my tears and started to snigger. With one look the man silenced them and slowly the crowd dispersed, except for my friends.

Megan and a friend I'd made in computer class called Georgia helped me up. Someone fetched Lauren and she came running over.

'We'll look after her,' they told the man.

'Okay,' he agreed.

'Thanks,' I gasped, trying to catch my breath.

The Headmaster was still there when we walked back into school. He couldn't get hold of Mum, so he telephoned my dad, who came straight away. Dad was furious when he saw the state of me. I was shaking and crying hysterically as the shock started to set in.

'Look at the state of her,' Dad said, his voice rising with anger. 'What on earth do you teach the kids here?'

He was standing in the corridor but he was shouting at the Headmaster.

'I can assure you, Mr Taylor...' the head began.

'Oh please, save your breath because I'm not interested. Look at my daughter. It's no wonder that girl didn't kill her! What sort of discipline do you have in this school anyway? None, by the look of it.' Dad's face was red with rage.

The Headmaster was speaking but he refused to listen.

'Come on, sweetheart,' he said, helping me to my feet. 'I'll take you back to Mum's, although God knows what she'll say when she sees the state of you.'

I didn't realise how bad my injuries were until I got home.

I looked in the bathroom mirror. My face was exactly the same but something inside had changed: the damage was hidden where no one could see.

Of course, Mum went crackers and shouted at Dad as if it was all his fault. It wasn't, but Mum was angry and had to take it out on someone.

'She's not going back to that school,' she ranted. 'Over my dead body!'

The attack had been completely unprovoked. I'd been humiliated a second time in front of what felt like the whole school. This was never going to end. It was only a matter of time before a third or fourth attack. The Head of Year had suspended the girl from school, but only for a few days.

Emotionally, I was a mess. I lived in fear of seeing her again, of coming face to face with her in the corridor. So when Mum said I didn't have to go back, I felt relieved.

'I'll speak to the authorities – there's no way you're going back there again.'

I felt glad that I wouldn't have to see the girl or my other tormentors but sad that I wouldn't see Lauren, Megan or Beth again either.

The attack stripped away what little confidence I had, and my already low self-esteem made me believe that I truly deserved it. Maybe I deserved to be beaten and abused by others. Maybe that's all I was good for and all I ever would be.

When Zeb called again and asked me to meet him I tried to refuse.

'No, I won't, because last time I did you hurt me,' I said, my voice trembling with fear.

Zeb sensed it and knew exactly what to say and do to get me to comply.

'Well, if you refuse to come to the house again, I'll just have to come and get you.'

'You don't know where I live,' I retorted.

But then he'd got hold of my mobile number; maybe he'd got my address too? I shook the thought from my head. Of course he didn't know where I lived.

'Don't I?' he whined. 'Let's see about that.'

The phone line went dead and he ended the call.

That's it, I thought to myself. *It's over. I said no, and now it's over.*

Only it wasn't. Moments later, my mobile rang again: it was Zeb.

'I know where you live,' he sang.

'No you don't,' I replied, but my mind was whirring. *Did* he know?

Then he repeated my full address, even my new postcode.

'How do you know that?' I gasped.

But Zeb just laughed.

'That's what you call contacts, love.' His voice was cold and menacing.

'Now meet me or I'll come and get you. If you don't, I'll come there and rape your mum. She'll get gang raped and I'll make you watch. Then,' he added, 'then it'll be your turn.'

There was a deathly silence as his threat hung in the air. He knew where I lived. If I didn't do as he said then he'd come and hurt Mum; he'd do to her what he'd done to me. I tried to speak but fear had stolen my voice.

'Meet me. Later, about 5pm. Usual place,' Zeb ordered.

The phone line went dead. I stared down at my mobile in horror. Did he mean it? Would he come for me? Would he rape Mum? I wasn't sure of anything anymore. All I knew was that

I was terrified of him. I was too scared to go but too frightened not to. I'd have to go, to protect Mum.

I watched the clock. Each second that ticked by felt like another step closer to Zeb. My heart was in my mouth. It was 4pm, only an hour to go until I met him again. He was the most frightening man I'd met in my entire life. I didn't want to go but I knew I had no choice. Fear gripped me as I glanced out of my bedroom window to the street below. It was a warm day and Mum and Phil were sat on the front lawn in the sunshine, chatting to our new neighbours. Mum had a glass of something in her hand. She laughed and smiled as she clinked it against Phil's glass. They looked as though they didn't have a care in the world; she looked so happy and in love. I shuddered when I thought about what Zeb had said he'd do to her if I didn't meet him.

At that moment, I watched from my upstairs window as two cars approached. They drove slowly along the street and, as they passed my house, they almost stopped as if on purpose. I spotted the men's faces – there were lots of them and they were all Asian. I didn't recognise them but I was certain it was Zeb. This was a warning. I had to do what he said. I couldn't risk it – he knew where I lived and he'd threatened Mum. I had no choice, I had to go.

My heart sank as I climbed into the back of Aban's car in the usual alleyway.

'Good girl,' said Zeb, turning in his seat to pat me on the knee. 'I knew you'd see sense.'

I trembled when I saw him.

'Please don't hurt me,' I begged.

Zeb looked at me in mock surprise.

'Of course I won't hurt you – I care for you, Katie. I'm going to take really good care of you. It'll be different this time,' he promised. 'I'll never hurt you again – that was a one-off. I'm here to look after you, to protect you. You want me to look after you, don't you, Katie?'

I nodded weakly. I wanted to be protected but I wanted protecting from him, not anyone else. I tried to process what he was saying. My mind raced because I wanted to believe him, but I couldn't forget what he'd done to me last time. The attack had left me fearful of everything and everyone; I had no confidence left. I felt as if life was carrying me along, with others making all the decisions for me. I'd have to do what Zeb said, otherwise I'd be punished. It was madness, of course, but I convinced myself that as long as I kept him happy, everything would be okay.

Only the second time wasn't different. He held me down in the secret house and raped me again. The only different thing was that I knew where we were going, and I knew he wouldn't kill me: Zeb wanted to have sex and he did so, again and again. It became so normal that I didn't even think of it as rape anymore because I'd let it happen. I'd let him do this to me and now I hated myself. Sex was all he'd ever wanted – he didn't care about me.

'Don't tell anyone about me or this house, understand?' he warned.

I nodded. I wouldn't dare because I knew if I did, worse things would happen. He'd hurt Mum and me. I knew that Zeb wasn't frightened of anyone – the only real fear he had was of being caught.

CHAPTER 14

MY NEW SCHOOL

'I'm sure you'll love it here, Katie.' The woman smiled as she shook my hand and led me into the new school.

It wasn't a big building and it didn't look like a school – it looked more like a prefab unit. It was all on one floor and ironically, given the fact that it was a school for problem teenagers, it was situated right next to the police station. Even though I'd not done anything wrong, I felt like a criminal just being there. But with no places available at other schools, I had very little choice. So, in the end, Mum had agreed.

The school was barren – only two classrooms and one office. The pupils were thin on the ground too; only five children including me.

'I'm sure you'll settle in fine,' the teacher said as she led me into the classroom.

There were four other teenagers in my class – two boys and two girls. They looked up at me as the door swung open and I stepped inside. Unlike my old school, you didn't have to wear a uniform. This school was more relaxed and friendly – you even got to call the teachers by their first names. It was odd, nothing like being at school at all.

The other kids were very unwelcoming. The girls were rough-looking; one was pregnant, although she was only fourteen, and the others were there because they'd been expelled from their previous schools. The boys wore tracksuits, flashy gold jewellery and trainers. One was so angry that he kept throwing stuff at the wall to see if he could smash it. I realised if I was to survive, I'd have to keep my head down. Suddenly, I felt very small.

Unlike normal schools, the lessons were taught on a one-to-one basis. I excelled at English but again I struggled with maths.

'She's proper thick,' the pregnant girl whispered to the others once the lesson had finished.

After that, the name-calling started all over again.

'Thick bitch,' the angry boy hissed. He picked up a pencil and threw it at my face like a dart. It hit the side of my cheek and I winced with pain.

I thought it'd been bad at my last school but this one was worse. At least I'd had a handful of friends before but now I was totally alone.

The bullying started and continued every time the teachers left the classroom. The others decided I was a loser. They took the mickey out of my hair and my clothes. Before I'd not worn the right skirt or school shoes but now I was ridiculed for wearing the wrong trainers – I'd never get it right.

'Watch out, here comes Loser!' one of the girls laughed.

I hated her, I hated them all.

The only bonus was my new school hours: we only did half

days and even then we were often given time off to study at home. To be honest, I think they thought we were a lost cause and once the teachers had done what they'd been paid to do, they couldn't wait to see the back of us.

One day I was sat in a lesson when my phone started to ring. I glanced down at the screen; it was Sam. I'd not heard from him in ages and I wondered how he'd been. At first I ignored it and turned it on 'silent', but it continued to light up with incoming text messages.

'Katie, can you turn your phone off, please?' my teacher sighed, her patience wearing thin. But I'd had enough of people telling me what to do and something snapped.

'I'm leaving,' I said, as I scraped my chair back against the floor and rose to my feet.

'But you can't just leave,' she said, trying to calm me down.

I looked around the classroom; the angry boy was pulling a face at me. I'd had enough.

'I don't want to stay here in this shitty school – I've had enough! I'm going to meet someone,' I shouted out loud.

'Who are you going to meet, Katie?' the teacher asked.

'A friend of mine – he's an Asian boy. He cares about me, not like you lot here!' The words blurted out as I grabbed my bag and headed for the door.

Five minutes later, my mobile rang: it was Dad. The school had called him and he wanted to meet me.

'I just want to talk,' he said.

I missed my dad so much that I agreed. I was standing opposite Sam's restaurant when I took the call. Sam was waiting for me but another few minutes wouldn't make much difference.

Five minutes later, Dad approached.

'I want to know who this lad is,' he demanded.

My mind raced; how did he know? Then it dawned on me – the teacher must've told him.

'He's my boyfriend,' I said.

'Well, I want to meet him, so where are you meeting him?'

Before I could stop them I felt my eyes dart over towards the Indian restaurant.

'Over there?' Dad said, taking my hand. 'Come on then, you can introduce me.'

With that he marched me across the road but the restaurant was closed.

Dad looked at me.

'Round the back,' I mumbled, signalling to the alleyway behind.

Sam's face clouded over when he saw the two of us approach. My heart was in my mouth – I didn't know what to say or do, I'd never seen my dad like this before.

'Are you Sam?' he asked, almost shouting at him.

Sam shook his head.

'No, I'm Nadeem – Sam's not here,' he lied.

My father swung to face me. His eyes were angry, his voice impatient.

'Is this the lad you're supposed to be meeting?'

I looked at Sam over Dad's shoulder. He shook his head and silently pleaded with me to say no.

'No, Dad, this is Nadeem. He's a friend of Sam's.'

I loved my dad and wasn't sure why I'd just lied to him. Sam was okay. He wasn't horrible like the others – Sam wasn't Zeb. But I was worried. If Dad found out about Sam, then he'd find out about the others too. He'd think I was a slag – he'd be ashamed of me.

'Are you sure this isn't Sam?' Dad asked again.

'Nope,' I replied, shaking my head. He wouldn't know.

'Well,' he said, turning back towards Sam, 'if you see this fella Sam, you can tell him that I'm looking for him and believe me, he doesn't ever want to meet me. This is my daughter and she's only fourteen years old. So you can tell your friend to stay away from her. Do you hear me?'

Sam looked terrified and I noticed that his hands were shaking by his sides.

'Yes, yes, I'll tell him,' he muttered, flustered.

Dad grabbed at my hand again.

'Come on, Katie, I'm taking you home.'

I tried to look behind to see Sam's face but Dad whisked me away.

He scolded me for mixing with older boys, but Sam was still a teenager. I knew then that I could never tell him about the others – they were older, they were all men.

After that, I never saw or heard from Sam again.

Zeb was curious about my new school and asked me lots of questions. We were sitting in the secret house when I began to tell him how much I hated it.

'And what time do you usually finish?' he asked, passing a joint to me. I took a drag.

'Dunno, it depends,' I said. 'Sometimes they let us go at lunchtime.'

Zeb pulled the joint from my fingers and took a long drag. He thought for a moment and then spoke.

'Nice,' he smiled.

I smiled too. I liked him when he was happy. Today was a good day; we'd met early and he was in a good mood.

My guard was down. He'd promised me alcohol and joints,

so I'd agreed to come. By now, I knew what to expect but I almost didn't care – my life was in freefall. At least Zeb showed me love.

Zeb walked over to the fridge and pulled out a couple of bottles of blue WKD – it was my favourite and he knew it.

As I gulped down the sweet and sickly blue liquid my head began to swim. Zeb leaned in and started to kiss my neck. It felt nice, gentle even.

'Things are going to be different, Katie,' he said, whispering in my ear.

'Me and you. Things will be good, I promise. Zeb just wants to take care of you.'

Before long, I'd drunk the bottle and Zeb handed me another. He lit up a joint and we smoked it all. Then he lit another. The drugs and alcohol gripped me; Zeb noticed and began to paw at my body.

'Here,' he said gently, lifting me to my feet, 'let's go upstairs.'

My legs felt heavy as he helped me to the white door at the bottom of the stairs. As he pulled the door open, I noticed something for the first time – a poster of a naked woman. I'd been at this house countless times but I'd never noticed the poster before. The woman looked cheap and tacky. Her head was missing from the picture; instead it showed her naked with her legs splayed open. The image turned my stomach. Even though my head was light and dizzy, the image of the woman stayed with me long after we'd climbed the stairs to the top floor. The more I thought about it, the more I shuddered. It was a horrible poster – really degrading, the sort a dirty old man would have on his bedroom wall. It was just a photograph of a woman's body – something to be used for sex – she wasn't even a real person anymore, just an object. Yet this was Zeb's house and it was on the door downstairs for everyone to see. I wondered why it was there; wasn't he embarrassed?

He pushed me down onto the bed and yanked down his trousers and boxer shorts. My body felt numb and I watched as he took out a condom and rolled it on himself. I felt as if I was looking through another pair of eyes, not my own – as though this was some sort of seedy porn film.

Moments later, with his bodyweight on top of me, I detached my mind from my body and allowed it to drift off. This wasn't happening to me – this was happening to someone else. It wasn't real; it was just in my head. It was the only way I could get through it.

I liked it when Zeb said nice things to me, when he nuzzled my neck with gentle kisses, when he told me how much he cared. I liked it when he bought me things, cigarettes and alcohol, and treated me like a grown-up. But I didn't like it when he pushed me down and forced me to have rough sex with him on the dirty mattress.

'Turn over,' he gasped.

He made me kneel on all fours and had sex with me from behind. The dirty mattress pressed against my face. The ingrained smell of sex in the fabric pressed up against my nostrils. Every time I breathed in I could smell it and I wanted to gag. It smelled of sex – dirty sex. Then it crossed my mind – I wondered how many other girls Zeb had brought here?

Afterwards, I longed for him to kiss and cuddle me but instead he ordered me to get dressed. He snapped his boxer shorts back on and the elastic pinged against his waist.

'You've got to go home now.'

He'd had his way and now he was finished with me. It made me feel cheap. I did as he said and pulled on my clothes, which were strewn across the floor. The fug in my head cleared as I fastened my bra.

Zeb put on his jumper and closed the door behind him. I heard footsteps on the stairs and then voices. As soon as I reached the bottom step, Aban was waiting for me with his hand resting on the latch of the front door.

'Ready?' he asked.

'Yes,' I nodded, my voice small and tight.

I'd thought Zeb loved me but he didn't, not really. I was only fourteen, almost fifteen years old, but I knew someone who loved you wouldn't treat you like this.

'Bye then,' I called to Zeb. I lifted my hand to wave goodbye but he didn't even look up.

'Yeah,' he mumbled as he flopped back down onto the sofa and flicked on the TV with the remote control.

Aban dropped me off in the alleyway and although it was still light, I ran all the way home. I passed Mum in the hallway; she was just leaving for work.

'Good day at school, love?'

'Yeah, great,' I lied.

Mum smiled and seemed relieved. She thought my life was back on track but it was far from it. If anything, it was in a downward spiral but I didn't know what to do to stop it. Closing my bedroom door behind me, I leaned against the wood and allowed the cool of the surface to soak through my clothes and into my back. I needed time to think but my head felt all scrambled.

Suddenly, my mobile vibrated in my jeans pocket. I pulled it out and I glanced at the screen. As I did, my heart sank – it was Wadi. I thought about not answering for a moment but I knew he'd pester me until I did.

'Hey, how's my favourite girl?' he asked, his voice light and bouncy

'I'm fine,' I lied, silent tears streaming down my face.

'It's just I haven't seen you for a while and…and well, I miss you. How about calling at the shop to see your old Wadi?'

'Err…' I said, trying to think of an excuse, but my mind went blank.

'Great, come round now if you like? I'm here and I'm looking forward to seeing you.' With that the phone line went dead.

My body ached. All I wanted was a good bath – a long, hot soak – but Wadi was waiting. I had to go. I cursed myself for not saying no. But instead, I pushed my mobile phone back into my pocket, wiped away the tears and headed downstairs to the front door. I'd reached a point where I couldn't say no. I was having sex with different Asian men but felt I had no choice. I was so naive – I'd gotten myself in too deep. I was trapped inside a deep pit of despair and there was no way out.

I hated myself, but at the same time I loved the attention they gave me. Stupidly, I mistook it for love.

That evening, Wadi had sex with me too, and the following day, Tali was on the phone again.

'I can't wait for us to live together, Katie. You know how much I love you and I want us to be together forever.'

I believed Tali when he said those things to me. I believed them all. I didn't stop to think that there was something seriously wrong with my life. I was having sex with all these different men yet I was still a child. None of this occurred to me because it had become my life. This was normal behaviour to me now. I was a dirty girl and I thought I didn't deserve any better – but I was wrong.

CHAPTER 15

A PIECE OF MEAT

I tried to avoid his calls but I knew I couldn't escape Zeb's clutches forever. One day I was walking home from school when a car drew up by the side of me. It was Zeb, but he was with another Asian man I'd never seen before – his name was Habis.

'Where have you been hiding?' asked Zeb.

My heart began to quicken. I'd seen that look on his face before and it scared me.

'You've not been answering your phone,' he scolded.

'It's been broken,' I lied. It was the first thing that came into my head.

Zeb studied me for a moment – I could tell he didn't believe me.

'I'll meet you around the back of the shop. Then you can get in the car,' he said.

I was too frightened to say no so I did as he said. It was a hot day and they'd had the roof of the car down, but as I approached they were pulling it back over.

'Why are you doing that – aren't you hot?' I asked, a little puzzled.

'Yes, but we can't be seen driving around town with a white girl, can we?'

Zeb's friend turned to face me. He was sitting in the driving seat but he smiled as he spoke.

'Especially not one who's as beautiful as you!' he gushed. 'Has anyone ever told you that you look just like Jennifer Lopez?'

I blushed. No one had ever said that to me before. Zeb noticed my face go red and it made him laugh.

'Come on, Hab, you don't have to be nice to her, just drive.'

Half an hour later we parked outside the secret house. I knew what was coming.

'Take Habis upstairs, Katie,' Zeb told me, so I did.

I'd never met Habis before but at least he was nice to me, nicer than Zeb. Habis called me beautiful. He said it again as we lay down on the mattress and had sex. It felt more normal, more equal somehow.

Afterwards, Zeb had sex with me too. This was how my life was. I was Zeb's girlfriend and that meant I had to do all these things to keep him happy.

Later we smoked a few joints and I drank lots of booze. I felt light-headed so I stumbled over to the sink, turned on the cold tap and splashed my face. The cool water felt good. I rubbed my face with a tea towel and stumbled backwards, but as I did, I felt something give behind me. Suddenly, my back went icy cold as though a frozen breeze had shot right through me.

Zeb saw and ran over to catch me.

'Whoa!' he shouted. I dipped back as he caught me in his arms and lifted me back to my feet. I turned to see him closing a door, one I'd never noticed before but one in the kitchen that seemed to lead down to a cellar.

'Where does that go?' I asked, catching a glimpse of the stone staircase leading down.

'Nowhere, it's nothing,' Zeb said, pulling me away.

'But I've never seen that door before,' I insisted. 'What's down there?'

Zeb got annoyed and started to lose his temper.

'It's nothing, okay? You must never, ever go down there, understand? There's nothing down there but you must never go down there or ask me about it again.'

'Okay, okay,' I said, putting my hands up in front of me to calm him down. 'I'm sorry, I won't ask again.'

I never did ask Zeb what was down there but I started to imagine all sorts of things. Were there other girls? What was he hiding and why had he got so upset? The thought of the mystery stairs unnerved me but I knew better than to ask about them again. I didn't want to upset Zeb because I didn't like him when he was angry.

A few days later he called and told me to meet him. I grabbed my bag.

'Where are you going?' Mum asked. By now, I was an expert at making things up.

'Lauren's.' I told her.

'Oh, okay.' Mum replied. I felt my heart break a little bit more. I was now fifteen and a typical teenager in many ways but I hated lying to her.

By the time I arrived, Aban's car was waiting. I expected him to drive us to the secret house, so I was a little confused when

Aban did a three-point turn in the middle of the main road and roared off in the opposite direction.

'Where are we going?' I asked.

'Work,' Zeb replied.

I shook my head. Zeb didn't work; he'd said he was a student. It didn't make sense but sure enough, five minutes later, we pulled up outside an office, which was situated in a small parade of shops. Zeb pulled out a set of keys I'd never seen before and unlocked a door around the back. He led me inside. The back room was filthy, with an old sofa and makeshift kitchen, but there was a door and it led through to a larger, cleaner-looking room with a desk, a chair and a telephone. It all looked very respectable. I wondered what kind of office it was but I knew better than to ask questions. There were slatted blinds in the front window and lots of paper on the desk. I wasn't sure what kind of place it was, but today it was obviously closed.

'Aban,' Zeb called. Aban looked up, nodded and headed out of the back door.

'Come here,' Zeb said, holding out his arms. I was nervous but I went to him. I didn't dare say no.

'Here,' he said, guiding my hand to the button of his jeans. They were tight and it was hard to undo the buttons but he breathed in and somehow I managed it.

'There,' he said, exposing himself. 'I want you to give me a blow job.'

'But…but…' I said, my voice beginning to quiver.

'Now,' Zeb ordered. He entwined my hair tight around his fingers and pulled my head back. Then he forced me down towards his crotch.

I was so frightened that I did as he said. Afterwards, he

dragged me into the back room of the office and had sex with me. The sex was rough and urgent. When he'd finished I watched as he pulled on his boxer shorts and fastened up his jeans. I automatically reached over for my clothes but Zeb grabbed my hand to stop me.

'Don't,' he hissed, 'you're not finished yet.'

Cold, frightened and naked, I wrapped my arms protectively around my chest as he walked out through the back door. I heard a car door slam and wondered where on earth he'd gone. Surely he'd not leave me here?

Moments later, the door swung open again and Aban stood in the doorway.

'Now you will have sex with me,' he said bluntly. I shook my head.

'Zeb says you must,' he insisted.

I was scared and vulnerable. I knew if I didn't do it, Zeb would come storming through the door at any minute and make me. It was easier to do as I was told.

Up until this point I'd thought maybe Aban was different. Sure, he'd driven me to these places but he'd never laid a finger upon me, until now. But even though he was frightened of Zeb, he was just as bad as him. And now that we'd had sex, I felt dirty and used, like a piece of meat.

Unlike Zeb, Aban didn't even use protection. I wondered if he hadn't been planning to have sex with me and had just grabbed the opportunity when it was presented. Zeb must have given him permission to do it – I was Zeb's possession, not Aban's. But now they were both using me.

Aban gasped as he sucked and licked at my breasts. I shut my eyes and suddenly I was back in the shop with Wadi. Only now it was Aban doing these disgusting things to me. Sweet, quiet

Aban – the man who wouldn't say boo to a goose. Yet here he was, pinning me down, having his way with me – he was just as bad as the others. I turned my head sideways so that he wouldn't see my tears.

I was a piece of meat to be used and abused. I existed not for myself, but solely for the use and enjoyment of others. Zeb had cheapened me and I'd allowed it to happen. I was fifteen years old but I didn't know how to make it stop; I was stuck in the middle of a nightmare.

Afterwards, as he pulled his trousers back on, Aban turned to me.

'I don't agree with all this, you know,' he said suddenly.

I wanted to slap him. He didn't agree with it? He'd just held me down and had sex with me. I couldn't even look at him.

'Look,' he said, grabbing me by the shoulders. 'I don't agree with what Zeb is doing to you but I can't stop him, Katie – no one can,' he insisted.

I lifted my head and looked into Aban's eyes. Deep down, I knew he wasn't a bad man – it was Zeb who was evil. His soul was blackened, just like his heart; he was rotten inside. Only bad things happened when Zeb was around. His whole world was seedy and disgusting. Aban was right; no one could stop Zeb. No one.

CHAPTER 16

MORE MEN ARRIVE

My mobile phone buzzed constantly. It didn't matter if I was at school, with Dean or at home. I was still seeing Dean and we still had sex occasionally but he was soon sick of all the texts and calls I was receiving. It made him paranoid and angry and before long it created a wedge in our relationship.

'Are you cheating on me?' he asked one day.

My eyes widened with horror.

'No, no…' I gasped – my voice sounded urgent and too defensive. It was clear something wasn't right. I jumped every time my phone pinged.

'I don't think I can do this anymore,' Dean said suddenly, shrugging me away. I wrapped my arms around his neck and tried to kiss him; he was the only good thing in my life right now.

'No, Katie. Leave me alone,' he snapped. 'Something's not right and I don't think I want to carry on. It's over.'

I put my hand to my throat to stop the hurt from welling up inside. Dean thought he knew but he didn't have any idea what I was going through. I tried to think how I could tell him. *I'm sleeping with all these different Asian men. They give me drink and drugs and, when I'm stoned, they have sex with me. I'm frightened but I don't know how to make it stop.* But even inside my head the words sounded horrible. They lodged high up in the back of my throat and refused to budge. Fear had simply locked them away.

'Okay,' I sniffed, 'if that's what you want.'

'It is,' Dean answered.

We were sitting by the lake and Dean got to his feet and zipped up his jacket.

'See you around, yeah?' he said, placing a hand gently on my shoulder. It made me feel even worse.

'Yeah,' I replied, staring off into the distance.

With that he left. I continued to stare at the lake – I wanted to throw myself in. I wanted to tie a heavy stone around my neck and allow the weight of it to drag me deep into the cold dark water. I'd sink to the bottom where I'd never be seen. The pain would leave my body and I'd be free. I'd be cold, dead and hidden and no one would ever be able to hurt me again.

I missed Dean dreadfully; he made me feel normal. But my life was far from that – it was full of phone calls and demands. Drained and exhausted, I found it hard to concentrate at school so I started bunking off. Not that anyone noticed or cared – I think I was beyond help. I drank and smoked too much hash and became a shadow of my former self. I felt less than worthless.

The cuts on my arm were mounting up and now there were scars upon scars. My wrists were constantly bloodied

with raised scars —for all to see if anyone had thought to look
— a cry for help. But I kept them hidden where no one would
find them.

One night, Zeb took me to the secret house but this time he
didn't seem bothered about having sex with me. For a moment
I wondered if I'd done something wrong and he was angry
with me. We always came to the house to have sex — it was
normal now. This wasn't.

'There's a guy called Hakim upstairs in the first bedroom,'
Zeb said. 'You should go up there and chill out with him.'

I took a swig from my bottle of WKD.

'But I don't know him,' I said, shaking my head.

'That doesn't matter. You need to get up there now.' Zeb's
voice was harsh. He handed me a joint and urged me to take a
drag. As I did, the weed slowly melted my brain.

'But what if I don't want to?' I slurred.

Zeb put down his bottle of beer and snatched the joint out
of my fingertips.

'You will do as I say!' he snapped, his eyes flashing with
anger. It scared me.

'Okay, okay,' I replied, backing off. He'd never hit me before
but I knew he was capable — he'd think nothing of it.

As I pulled open the door with the dirty poster on it, things
became clearer. He didn't want to see the woman's face in the
poster because he didn't want to see who she was. He just saw her
body — something to be used. As all these thoughts entered my
head, Zeb suddenly called my name. The sheer sound of his voice
jolted me with fear and brought me back into the moment.

'Here,' he said, handing me a few rolled-up joints, 'take
these.'

I looked at them in my hand and guessed these were what I'd use to 'chill out'.

'Now go on, be a good girl for Zeb. Hakim is waiting.'

I did as Zeb asked and climbed the stairs. I knew that I wasn't going to that bedroom to 'chill out' – I'd been sent up there to have sex with a man I didn't even know. And I'd do it. I'd do it because I was frightened of Zeb and what he'd do to me.

The man was skinny and smelt of body odour. He had buck teeth that stuck out when he smiled. I felt my stomach lurch because he was so ugly. I guessed he was in his early thirties but he was dressed like a tramp, wearing a horrible scruffy T-shirt with stains down the front.

He didn't pull any punches. We'd only smoked one spliff between us when he pounced on me. We were in the lower-floor bedroom, which also had a bed in it. Like the room at the top of the house, the mattress was stained and unmade. I just wanted to get it over and done with as quickly as possible. The thought of driving home in Aban's car kept me going as I allowed my mind to drift off.

A week later, Zeb took me to the secret house but this time Habis was waiting for me. I felt relieved because at least I'd met him before – he wasn't a stranger.

Zeb ignored me and walked through to the back of the house and opened up the fridge. The men drank beer whilst I guzzled down bottles of alcopops. Zeb lit up a joint and we all took a drag. I thought that tonight, because we were in the living room, I'd not have to do anything. Unlike Hakim, Habis made no attempt to go upstairs to the bedroom on the first floor. I thought I was safe, but I was wrong.

After half an hour of drinking, talking and smoking joints, Zeb rose to his feet.

'I'm going to clean up,' he announced.

I was flabbergasted because I'd never seen Zeb do anything domestic before. I watched in amazement as he went through to the kitchen and came back in, holding a damp cloth in his hand. He then proceeded to dust down the surfaces. It was only later that I realised perhaps he was doing this to wipe away our fingerprints – traces of us having been there.

'Katie,' Zeb said, his back turned to me as he sorted through some papers on the coffee table. 'I want you to give Habis a blow job.'

I looked at Zeb in shock but he refused to look at me. Instead I glanced over at Habis. I expected him to be shocked, to say something, but he just grinned back as if this had been the plan all along.

I opened my mouth to speak but no words came out; instead I sat in numbed silence.

'Katie,' Zeb said, turning to face me, 'I said give Habis a blow job NOW!'

He was so angry that he spat out the words and his eyes flashed with fury. My heart thudded inside my chest. I wanted to scream 'No!' Every fibre of my body told me to bolt for the door and to keep on running until I'd made it back home. But the secret house was miles away. I was trapped; no one even knew I was here. I was all alone.

My hands trembled as I lifted myself up from the sofa and made my way across the room to where Habis was sitting. He saw me approach and unzipped his trousers in anticipation.

'Good girl,' Zeb muttered as he turned back to the cleaning.

I performed oral sex on Habis but my eyes darted sideways

to see where Zeb was. I expected him to leave the room but he didn't. Instead he moved around, tidying up as if this was the most normal thing in the world. I'd done things for Zeb, I'd had sex with his friends, but this was the first time I'd done something like this in front of him – as though I was performing for his amusement. I felt cheap and embarrassed at the same time.

That night when I got home I brushed my teeth again and again until the gums bled. Afterwards, I swilled neat mouthwash around. It stung at cuts inside my mouth but I didn't care – it was making me clean again. Only then did I feel hygienic enough to eat my dinner, but even then the food lodged inside my throat. My body wouldn't let me eat because I felt so repulsed by the men, but most of all, I felt repulsed by myself.

After that day, it became normal practice for me to perform blow jobs or have sex with random men just to please Zeb. By doing it, I knew I was keeping him happy – and when he was happy, he was kind to me. I reminded myself that I was doing this to protect Mum.

It got to the point where sex with strangers was happening two or three times a week and I never knew who would be there when I opened the door. To get through it I drank and smoked more and more. It blurred everything into one big jumbled mess and numbed both the physical and emotional pain. It also stopped something else – it stopped me from thinking for myself.

One night, Aban drove me over to the house. I'd only been there for a matter of minutes when there was a knock at the front door. Both men momentarily froze and looked up at one another. I went to speak, but Zeb held his hand up to stop me. Silently, he drew a finger against his lips and tip-toed over to the window to see who it was. With a pointed finger he signalled to Aban to take me upstairs, where we sat on the bed in the first bedroom. I waited for Aban to touch me or try something but he didn't. Instead he listened intently as Zeb opened the front door.

Although it was muffled and hard to hear, I could just about make out the voice of a girl. She sounded young – she sounded just like me. There was laughter. The front door closed as I heard Zeb invite her inside. Moments later, there was the sound of bottles clinking and laughter. Suddenly everything went quiet – my mind raced. What were they doing? And then it hit me: they were having sex.

I tried to stand up but Aban pulled me back down onto the side of the bed. He hissed at me to be quiet. We remained like that for at least half an hour. Then I heard the sound of laughter and long, protracted goodbyes. There were girl's footsteps out in the street as heels clicked along the pavement and off into the night. Only then did Aban let me move or talk.

Zeb called up to us to tell us the coast was clear.

'Who was that?' I demanded to know as soon as I reached the living room. I felt strangely annoyed that Zeb had another girlfriend besides me. But he stood there and just shrugged his shoulders.

'It was no one,' he replied.

I knew he was lying. I wanted to know who it was; a weird sense of jealousy welled up inside me and took me by surprise. I didn't love Zeb, I was frightened of him but I also didn't like the idea of being one of many girls. It made me feel even cheaper. My head was a mess – it was so scrambled with drink and drugs I didn't know what to think or feel anymore.

'Okay,' said Zeb, holding up his hands in defeat. 'It was my ex-girlfriend. She came here tonight because she wanted to have sex. Now are you satisfied?'

I nodded blankly. I didn't know what to believe anymore.

A few nights later, we drove to the house but this time there was only me, Zeb, Aban and a man called Jad. I guessed it was a nickname or a shortening of something else.

Zeb walked straight over to the fridge but instead of WKD, he poured me something else.

'What is it?' I asked, eying the glass suspiciously as he handed it over.

'It's a vodka and Coke; I've run out of the other stuff,' he said. He raised his bottle of beer and clinked it against the tumbler in my hand.

I nodded and took a small sip of the brown liquid just to be sure. It tasted okay – it tasted of Coke. I allowed myself to relax. I drank another one and then another. My head was light when Zeb called me over. He pulled me down onto his lap and started to undo my top. But there were others in the room and I didn't like it. I wanted Zeb to stop but I didn't know how to ask because I didn't want him to turn nasty. There were three of them and only one of me.

My head felt fuggy as I felt fabric slip against my skin. I glanced down to see my top in his hands. His fingers snaked across my back as he fumbled, trying to unclip my bra. I looked up at him with pleading eyes. I didn't mind sex with him but I didn't want to be naked here, not in front of everyone.

'Sssshall we go upstairs?' I asked. I cringed inwardly as I heard my own voice slurring the words. The vodka was stronger than I thought.

'No,' Zeb insisted.

I felt a tug and with one hand he pulled off my bra. My top

half was naked for all to see. I felt vulnerable and wrapped my arms around myself.

'No, don't do that, we can't see you properly if you do that,' Zeb teased, pulling my arms clear of my breasts.

Aban laughed, but Jad didn't.

'Leave her alone!' Jad snapped.

Zeb shot him a stern look and Jad backed down. Then he laughed and pretended that he'd not meant it.

Soon Zeb was unbuttoning and pulling at my jeans.

'But I don't want to,' I said, trying to hitch them back up again.

'You do love me, don't you?' Zeb asked, his eyes wide with surprise.

'Yes,' I whispered.

'Well, let me do this then,' he coaxed. A wave hit my body and I felt myself slump in his arms. It was the alcohol kicking in some more, numbing my body.

Seconds later, Zeb pulled off my jeans and my clothes lay in a dishevelled heap in the middle of the floor.

The room was spinning and I felt disorientated as I tried to climb off his lap to get to my clothes. My eyes darted from one man to another. I protectively clamped my arms against me in an attempt to cover myself up. But Zeb, Aban and Jad sat there and did nothing. Instead they just sniggered – I was the entertainment.

'Please don't,' I begged, beginning to weep.

I felt a tug behind me. I turned to see Jad standing there. He had his fingers hooked through the back of my G-string and he was trying to pull my knickers off.

'No!' I hissed, lashing out at him.

'I won't do this anymore!' I screamed at Zeb with tears in my eyes.

The moment had come – I'd found the courage to say no. I was sick of Zeb telling me what to do, treating me like an animal. I realised I didn't have to do this anymore. I didn't have to let him hurt me. Nothing he could do to me could be any worse than this.

Zeb got to his feet and stood in front of me. His body towered over mine and I suddenly felt very small. My body trembled when I saw the hateful look in his eyes.

'You must do as I say,' he said, grabbing my arm roughly.

'No,' I replied. I heard my voice crumble and weaken. 'I won't do it, not anymore and you can't make me.'

Zeb's eyes flashed with anger. A bolt of terror shot through my body as I felt the thud-thud of my heart.

'Ah, but you're wrong because I *can* make you do these things for me and I *will*.'

I looked over at the others to say something but they didn't. Instead they sat there, mute.

'You're forgetting something, Katie. I know where you live…' Zeb continued, '…and who your mother is.'

'I'll go and see her. I'll rape her and make you watch while I do it.'

'You wouldn't,' I challenged. But I believed every word – he said he'd do anything to get what he wanted.

'Try me,' he hissed.

For a moment the room was silent. All I could hear was my own breath. I gasped for air to try and calm my pounding heart.

Someone laughed and broke the silence and the room returned to normal. I thought about Mum. If I didn't do as he asked, Zeb was sure to hurt her. I was determined they wouldn't ruin her life as they had mine.

Instead I reached to the coffee table for my glass and gulped down the rest of my drink. Alcohol was good – it numbed the pain and blocked things off.

I faced Zeb and as I did, I felt another tug from behind and felt something slide down between my legs. I looked down in horror to see my knickers on the floor between my feet.

Jad punched the air jubilantly as if he'd just scored a goal and the others cheered.

Hot and humiliated, I dipped down and pulled up my pants. They continued to cheer and wolf whistle me and I felt dirty and used.

'Here,' Zeb said in a gentle voice.

He held out his arms and I ran to him so that he would cover me up. I shut my eyes to block them all out. I felt safe in Zeb's warm embrace. He was in charge – if anyone could protect me, it'd be him. But seconds later, he pushed me roughly back into the centre of the room. Then he started to undo his jeans.

'Give me a blow job,' he demanded.

'But…I…' I gestured with my eyes to the others sitting there. They were watching my every move but Zeb didn't care.

'Give me a blow job,' he shouted. 'Give me one NOW!'

I shut my eyes so I wouldn't see them. Instead I allowed a numbness to wash over me as I knelt down and did exactly as Zeb had asked.

A few minutes later, Zeb pulled away from me.

I was handed another drink. It tasted of Coke and something else – probably vodka, I couldn't tell. The alcohol slid down the back of my throat and I gulped at it greedily. Then I was given another and another.

The room started to spin again. I flopped onto the sofa to make it keep still but it wouldn't stop turning.

'Stand up, Katie.' I heard a voice – it was Zeb's.

He was trying to pull me back to my feet but my head was woozy and my body felt as heavy as lead. Suddenly, my knees gave way and I crashed down hard onto the floor. Hands reached out, pulling and lifting me back to my feet again. Somehow, with someone pulling and someone pushing from behind, I managed to climb the stairs. When I came round, I realised I was lying on the bed in the top bedroom. Zeb, Aban and Jad were standing next to me in a line. I felt disorientated and confused. Zeb's voice broke through the fog in my head.

'You have to give us all blow jobs,' he ordered.

But I felt sick; the room was spinning and I wanted it to stop. 'I *can't!*' I begged.

Out of nowhere, a hand grabbed me around the back of my head and forced my face downwards. It was Zeb. He would make me do this whether I wanted to or not. After a few moments, he pulled my head away and forced it onto Aban and then Jad. This sick sexual merry-go-round continued as I was forced to perform oral sex on each and every one of them.

Zeb threw me back and wearily I flopped down onto the bed. My head was throbbing. Bile rose up from my stomach into my throat until I could contain it no longer. I threw up all over the filthy mattress whilst they stood and watched. Thinking my ordeal was over I vomited a second time. I shut my eyes, my mind closed down and everything went black. I don't know how long I was unconscious but when I woke up, I was in Zeb's arms. He held me tenderly as though he really cared.

'Katie, can you hear me? I'm so sorry.' It was Zeb's voice. Even in my dazed state I thought how odd it was to hear him say the word 'sorry'. Yet he said it again and again.

I tried to move my legs but couldn't feel them – I began to panic.

'Pleassse helpppp meeee!' I begged. My voice sounded alien as the words slurred out from my mouth. My head was spinning out of control but my body felt as dead as a lump of wood.

'I can't move my legs – there's something wrong,' I cried.

I saw Jad panic. He ran off downstairs to fetch me a bottle of water. Moments later, he reappeared and Zeb snatched the bottle from him. Holding back my head, Zeb poured the water straight down my throat. My whole body convulsed as I started to choke. Water spluttered everywhere as I coughed and gasped for breath. I thought Zeb would go mad but he just stared – his eyes were full of concern.

I was confused but I sensed a rising panic in the room. My mind drifted in and out as voices blurred and they spoke in echoes. My jumbled mind struggled as it tried to process what they were saying.

Jad was speaking too quickly; I opened my eyes and saw his arms flailing about. He looked anxious and was arguing with Zeb.

'She needs to go to hospital – we've got to get her there quick,' he insisted. Zeb refused.

'Don't be stupid; we can't take her! If we do then they'll know what we've been doing.'

I wondered what he meant but my mind shut down. I needed to rest, to sleep. I needed to switch off. Somewhere, in the back of my mind, I recalled the blow jobs and shuddered. I tried to move again but my legs felt heavy and totally unconnected to my body.

Zeb continued to cradle me in his arms. He told me how much he loved me. I wanted to believe him, but why did I feel so dead?

Eventually, I felt coldness set in against my skin and the numbness wore off. My body felt stiff and broken. I knew I was in Zeb's arms and assumed I was still on the bed but then I realised that I was actually on the floor. As feeling flooded back into my body I moved my legs but an unexpected pain ripped through me. It was so intense that it stole my breath away. I glanced down and saw that I was completely naked. I moved my legs a second time but the excruciating pain shot through me once more. As I looked down I realised the soreness was coming from between my legs.

My eyes darted to the side. I spotted my G-string on the floor. They must have ripped my knickers off again when I passed out. Although my head was woozy, I slowly pieced things back together. I looked across the room. There was no one else in there now, only me and Zeb.

'Where am I?' I asked him.

'I'm sorry, Katie, I'm so sorry,' he said over and over.

'I'll look after you, I promise,' he told me. His voice was different – he sounded frightened. I'd never heard Zeb sound frightened before.

Wrapping his arms around me, he lifted me back onto the bed. He walked away to the corner of the room. When he got closer to me I saw he was holding something in his hands – my clothes. I was confused because I knew he'd undressed me downstairs.

I tried to get dressed but something was wrong, the pain was too intense. I felt raw and burnt down below, as though someone had scalded me internally. Eventually I managed, with Zeb's help, to pull on my clothes. He helped me to my feet as gingerly I placed one foot in front of the other. But the pain was severe and I winced with every step I took. Gently, Zeb led me back downstairs. I was puzzled; why was he being so nice? It didn't make sense.

When I finally reached the last step and turned into the living room I suddenly understood: the room was full of men. There were at least five others I'd never seen before. I looked up at them but no one would look at me. As soon as I entered the room they stopped talking. Apart from Zeb, Aban and Jad, I'd never met any of them before.

'Who are they?' I asked Zeb, my body shaky and unstable.

But Zeb wouldn't answer. Instead, one by one, the men left until there was only me, Zeb, Aban and Jad. But still no one spoke. It made me feel worse, as though something awful had just happened.

Suddenly, Zeb broke the silence.

'Aban will take you home now, Katie. You need to go home and rest, do you hear me?'

I nodded but my body felt broken. And then it dawned on me: I was sore, battered and bruised because all those men had just had sex with me. I'd been a gang-raped. I'd passed out but I wasn't stupid; they'd violated me whilst I'd been unconscious. They'd done this to me.

I suddenly thought of the sofa in the bedroom. When you sat down on it you had a full view of the double bed – it was almost like a viewing platform. I wondered if these men had sat there, one by one, to watch events unfolding like some sick and perverted sex show. I hadn't consented to any of this; not even through fear. I'd passed out on the bed and I'd been raped, probably by all of them. My whole body shuddered with revulsion and I felt the bile rise and burn inside my throat once more.

As the car sped away I looked out of the back window and

stared into the darkness. Now my soul felt as black as the night. I'd been poisoned by Zeb – he was evil, a monster. I was his property and I'd never escape him, not ever. This was my life now – it was all I knew.

CHAPTER 17

THE BABY

'Are you okay?' Mum asked. It had been a few months since I'd been gang raped and it had left me feeling sick and rotten inside.

I was still seeing Zeb and although I never saw the strange men from that night again, he was still making me have sex with different people even when I didn't want to. I didn't feel like a person anymore – I was just a sex toy. I was there to be used and abused by him and his acquaintances. I wasn't Katie anymore, I was just an object – *his* object. Every part of me, from my head to my toes, was there for his pleasure. My mouth was there to perform blow jobs, my breasts were there to be groped, and down below was there for him or whoever he 'gave' me to, to enjoy. My body wasn't my own anymore – it belonged to Zeb and he made me feel disgusting. I didn't feel like a human being. He controlled me now; he was the boss.

I cut myself more and more. It was the only thing I had control of as every other aspect of my life slowly spiralled out of control. Part of me hoped that one day I'd even manage to sever through a main artery – at least then it'd all be over and I wouldn't have to face Zeb again. I hoped I'd have the guts to slice right through my lifeline, to end it all with one last cry for help. I dreamed about it constantly; I'd lay there and watch the blood gush from my body, my life ebbing away in a flood of pain. I was still only fifteen years old it but felt as if my life was already over – I wanted to die.

Mum was still watching, eyeing me cautiously from the other end of the kitchen. I knew I looked pale and puffy – my eyes were swollen through lack of sleep and too much alcohol. I was struggling to cope in more ways than one. I constantly felt hungover and wretched; I was dirty, both inside and out. Some days I felt so bad that I thought my skin would crawl clean off my body.

'You don't look right; you look a bit pale to me,' she insisted, pressing a cool hand against my forehead. 'You definitely look a bit peaky.'

'I'm fine,' I lied, shrugging her away. I wanted to tell her about the men, about the secret house, the drugs, the alcohol, and the sex. The sex. My stomach flipped at the thought of it. How could I tell her? She'd be disgusted with me. She'd call me a dirty little slag and she'd be right. Maybe that's all I was now? Maybe I deserved this? Deep down I somehow knew I was being ridiculous but that's how Zeb made me feel – worthless.

No, I reasoned. I'd be fine as long as I did everything Zeb said. But the truth was I wasn't fine. Mum was right, I was sick – something was wrong. Normally the smell of her cooking would make my mouth water but now it made me want to vomit. Sometimes even a cup of tea was enough to set me off; I couldn't help it. Maybe this was my punishment for doing all these things. Maybe I was now so disgusting that I repulsed myself.

Mum was still watching me. She didn't look convinced that I was okay.

'Okay. But you'll tell me if you don't feel well, won't you?' she insisted.

I nodded weakly.

'Good girl,' she said.

I got up from where I was sitting, and wandered back upstairs to my bedroom. My heart sank at the thought of the day ahead. I knew that as soon as I left school, Zeb would be waiting. The thought of him made my heart race and my palms sweat. He was a dangerous man. I was certain he had bigger plans for me; I just didn't know what they were yet.

When my mobile buzzed later that day, it took all the strength I had to answer it. I forced my voice so it sounded bright and breezy, I didn't want to annoy him.

'Meet me in an hour. Usual place,' he said. The phone clicked off and he'd gone.

By now I was having sex with different men almost every night of the week. They were usually friends of Zeb's, and he told me it was alright. I had sex with Hakim and gave him blow jobs. I also had sex a few times with Habis and Jad. Jad asked me to meet him on my own but I was worried there might be another secret house, so I refused. He was pissed off but I knew my body couldn't cope with much more. At least with Zeb in charge he wouldn't force me to have sex with anyone he didn't trust.

Even so, I was still frightened of Zeb – too frightened not to go along with his plans. If I said no, he'd hurt me for sure.

That night I travelled to the secret house in Aban's car. There was the usual blur of men's faces waiting as the front door closed behind me. I gulped down the vodka and Coke that Zeb handed to me. Alcohol was good, it was my medicine – it numbed my body and mind. The hash helped too. It blocked things out. As long as I got smashed on dope everything would be okay. I wouldn't be able to feel it and, if I drank enough booze, I'd get blanks in my memory and wouldn't be able to fill things in later on.

As the night progressed, I performed oral sex on several different men and lay down on the old stained mattress whilst they each took it in turns to have sex with me. By now I knew that mattress so well; every inch of the fabric, every stain was etched into my mind like a familiar old pattern.

I tried not to think too much about things. Zeb insisted he was my real boyfriend and that he'd take care of me. This was normal, he told me. He said that you did things you didn't want to do – you made sacrifices for the one you loved. Deep down, I knew I didn't love Zeb: I was frightened of him. That wasn't love, it was fear. But it was also my life. I didn't like it, but it was all I knew. I'd just have to get used to it – I'd have to learn to like it because I couldn't bear to think of the consequences if I dared to say no.

My mind was so fuzzy with spliffs and booze that I'd not noticed my period was late. I hadn't had one at all for quite a while. Normally, they were as regular as clockwork but I'd had nothing, no pain. Instead I'd felt odd and constantly sick.

Oh my God! I suddenly shuddered. I knew it could mean only one thing.

That afternoon, I walked to a chemist's shop at the other end of town. The woman spotted me from behind the counter as soon as I pushed open the door and I felt her eyes on me as I wandered over to a stack of shelves in the middle of the shop.

My eyes darted around me. There was an old woman in the corner talking to the pharmacist about her various ailments. I didn't know her. There was another woman soothing a crying baby in her arms. She looked as though she was waiting to speak to the pharmacist too. Her eyes rolled impatiently and she glanced at her watch. She was annoyed – the old lady was taking too long and the baby was fractious. I didn't know either of them. I sighed with relief.

'Can I help you?' a voice called.

It was the assistant behind the counter. The woman with the baby looked up and I felt my face flush.

'Um, no, I'm just looking,' I mumbled. I pretended to walk around the display, looking for something that didn't exist. Anything other than what I'd really gone there for. But it was no good: I had to do this – I *had* to know.

I walked back to the other side of the display and glanced at the prices. There was one for 99p – a bargain. It looked pretty basic but at least I could afford it. The others were way out of my league. Grabbing the cheap pregnancy test kit, I made for the counter and handed it to the woman with some money. I tried not to look at her but I could feel her staring – her eyes burning into me. She knew I was too young to be buying a pregnancy test kit.

She popped it inside a paper bag and handed it to me with my change and a till receipt. The receipt said exactly what I'd bought. I screwed it up into a ball in my hand and threw it in the nearest bin outside.

Back at home I locked myself in the bathroom, pulled it from the packet and quickly read the instructions. One line for 'not pregnant', two for 'pregnant'. I prayed for just the one. The blue stripe appeared almost immediately. I sighed with relief – I was in the clear. I heard Phil pottering around downstairs so I tucked the pregnancy wand up my sleeve and headed back to my bedroom. But a few minutes later, a second line began to appear. Frantically, I read the instructions again but they shook in my hands. I burst into tears. What the hell was I going to do? Suddenly, there was a knock at my bedroom door; it was Phil.

'Katie? I need to come in. The boiler's not working and I need to have a look at it.'

I ran to the door and grabbed at the handle – I had to stop him coming in.

'But you *can't*,' I gasped.

I shoved my whole body weight against the door to buy myself more time. I glanced across the room and then at the pregnancy wand in my hand – I didn't even have time to hide it.

'Katie, open the door NOW!' Phil shouted. He sounded annoyed. 'I need to fix the boiler.'

I felt my heart stop; I had no choice. I opened the door and began to cry.

'Phil, I've just done a pregnancy test. I'm pregnant!'

He reeled back in horror and steadied himself against the wall.

'*What*?' he exclaimed. Then he began to laugh as if it was a joke. His laughter made me weep more and soon he realised I wasn't joking; this was real.

'I'm pregnant,' I said, repeating the words.

Phil ran his fingers through his hair as if he needed time to think. He knew he'd have to tell Mum.

'Oh my God, Katie!' he gasped.

But I couldn't speak. My secret was out and there was nothing I could do.

Later that night, Phil told Mum. I heard her cry downstairs and it made me feel even worse. I picked up my mobile and dialled a number.

'Dean,' I said, 'I'm pregnant.'

Dean heard the word and began to panic.

'But I'm too young to be a dad. We can't have this baby, Katie – we're too young.'

At first I didn't think about what he was saying and then I realised; he thought the baby was his. Suddenly, it dawned on me: this could be my escape route. If he thought it then Mum would too and my secret would be safe and they wouldn't have to know about Zeb or the others.

Mum came up to my bedroom to speak to me. Her face was stained with tears and she looked crushed with disappointment.

'You and Dean,' she began. 'You're too young to be parents – you have your whole lives ahead of you.'

Inwardly, I sighed. She thought the baby was Dean's too. I hadn't lied to either of them, they'd just assumed it. If they wanted to believe it then I'd let them.

Hours later there was a knock at the door: it was Dean. Mum showed him in, but she didn't say much. The atmosphere was stiff and awkward.

'She's in her room,' I heard her say.

Dean came up to my bedroom but I could barely look at him for all the guilt I felt inside. He sat down on the bed next to me.

'We can't have this baby, Katie. We're too young…' he began. I looked at him but my guilty expression gave me away. I couldn't do this anymore. I couldn't lie to Dean, he didn't deserve it. It took a moment for the penny to drop but suddenly his face changed. He stood up and backed away from me in horror.

'It *is* my baby, isn't it?'

I shrugged my shoulders. I thought of all the men I'd had sex with; how many had used protection and how many hadn't.

'It could be yours or up to eight different men,' I replied coldly.

Dean reeled back as though I'd just smacked him in the face. He looked mortified.

'I *knew* it!' he said. 'I *knew* you were cheating on me!'

I didn't have to see his eyes to know that he was disgusted – I could hear it in his voice.

'I…I didn't, it's just that…' I said, suddenly searching for the right words.

'But you must have, Katie! You must've cheated on me – I can't believe it!'

He was pacing around the room, trying to take it all in. Suddenly, he shot me one last look of disgust and headed for the door. I heard it slam behind him as he ran downstairs and out into the street. I'd almost told him everything, but I'd managed to stop myself.

That evening, when Zeb called me I ignored my phone. I didn't want to talk to him or anyone else; I just wanted to be alone. For a split second I thought about ringing up Lauren, but what would I tell her? She'd want to know who the father was and what would I say? I didn't even know myself; as I'd told Dean, it could be one of many men.

The following day, Mum had the same old conversation with me about being too young to raise a child. By now her tears had turned to anger.

THE BABY

'I'm sorry,' I mumbled.

Mum tutted and placed her hands flat on the kitchen table.

'It's too late for sorry, Katie,' she said, her voice tight and stiff. 'You're not keeping it and you can tell Dean that I said so.'

I chose not to correct her. If she still thought this baby was Dean's then I'd let her.

'But I want to keep it! It's not the baby's fault – it didn't ask to be born,' I wailed.

I couldn't help it. Overnight I'd become attached to the life growing inside me. Until now my life had been sad and empty, but this baby might be my chance to turn things around. Maybe it was meant to be.

'I just want to love and protect it,' I sobbed.

Mum sighed heavily and took my hand in hers.

'Look, Katie, how would you support it? You're too young – it would take over your life. You wouldn't be able to provide for it,' she said, her voice softening.

Her anger, like her tears, began to subside as she tried her best to help me work things out.

'What about if I have the baby and put it up for adoption?' I suggested, the idea popping into my head.

Mum shook her head.

'Katie, it would be even harder for you to give birth to a baby and hand it over – that would crucify you for the rest of your life. It would haunt you. You need to get rid of this baby and you need to do it sooner, rather than later. The longer you leave it, the harder it'll get.'

I knew that Mum was only saying these things because she was looking out for me but I wondered how much joy a baby would bring to my life. Of course, I knew I'd have to tell them

217

about Dean not being the father. They'd be able to tell anyway, by the colour of the baby's skin.

'I'm not getting rid of it,' I decided, getting to my feet. 'This is a life growing inside me and it doesn't have anyone but me to look after it. You can't ask me to kill it.'

With that, I turned and went upstairs to my bedroom.

I felt trapped. I wanted to have this baby but if I did, the colour of his skin would betray me.

Dean had almost always used protection so there was very little chance of it being his. Deep down, I knew the baby wasn't his, and soon the whole world would know too. I wanted to have the baby but if I did everyone would discover my secret. And, if I did as Mum said then everything would be fine: Dean would be off the hook, no one would know about me and my secret, and I'd be able to go on living my life. With a heavy heart, I went back downstairs and spoke to Mum.

'Okay, okay,' I said wearily. 'I'll have an abortion.'

She sighed with relief.

'Okay, I'll sort everything out, make the necessary phone calls,' she said briskly. Her voice sounded cold, almost businesslike.

I knew I was killing a life just to save mine and it felt all wrong. I hated myself for it – I felt guilty and as rotten and evil as the men who'd done this to me.

CHAPTER 18

THE ABORTION

Mum and I travelled to the nearest city to an abortion clinic. 'Ready?' she asked, as we climbed out of Phil's car.

'Ready,' I said, but I knew I wasn't and that I never would be. I'd worked out that I was roughly ten weeks pregnant and as my stomach hardened and swelled, I started to feel it.

Mum gave my name at reception and we walked through into a waiting area. I tried not to look at the other girls in there but I couldn't help it. One looked even younger than me. I wondered what had gone so wrong in her life that she'd ended up there. Most were older, though, in their late teens or early twenties. Some were flicking through magazines whilst others just stared straight ahead. Others were fidgeting, playing nervously with mobile phones.

The place was bright and modern. They'd tried to spruce it up with homely things – a few plants, nice pictures on the walls, comfy chairs – but we all knew the real reason we were there.

Before long, a nurse came out and called my name and I was taken to a room for a consultation with another member of staff. As she led me along the corridor I felt Mum's eyes burning into my back from the waiting room, pleading with me to give the right answers.

The nurse asked me lots of questions, including why I wanted an abortion.

'I don't know,' I whispered truthfully.

The nurse sighed and placed her pen on the desk.

'You don't have to do this if you don't want to. This is your choice and you can change your mind at any time,' she explained gently.

I wanted to weep. It was as though she'd read my mind. I didn't want to be here, sat in this room, about to kill my baby. But I couldn't have it either. If I gave birth, everyone would know I'd slept with Asian men. Everyone would find out – I felt I had no choice.

'Katie, this is really important,' the nurse told me. 'If you have any doubts about the abortion then you shouldn't do it. You must go away and think long and hard about what it is you really want.'

My head was telling me one thing but my heart was saying quite another.

'Katie, we cannot perform an abortion unless I'm absolutely convinced it is what you want, do you understand?'

I panicked when I realised she might say no. I got up and fled the room. Mum saw me in the corridor and came running over. When I told her what the nurse had said, she went mental.

'Listen, you *have* to do this! I'll not let you ruin your life,' she insisted. Mum held my head in her hands. 'Now you go back in there and tell her what she wants to hear.'

I knew she was right. By killing my baby I'd save my own neck – but that didn't make it right. In fact, it made it worse.

The clinic was small. Mum wasn't allowed to come into the treatment room with me so I was all alone. In a way I wanted her there. Perhaps if she was I'd be able to get her to change her mind and make her realise that we'd get through it; she'd let me keep my baby. But I'd have to tell her my secret and then everyone would know, even Dad. My heart sank. No, I had to do this – I'd have to kill my baby to make everything alright again.

As I signed my signature on the consent form I thought my heart would break in two. My hand shook as I gripped the pen. By signing it I was giving these people permission to kill my unborn child.

I was given an ultrasound scan to assess how pregnant I was but I didn't look. The nurse turned the screen away anyway, and I didn't ask her to turn it back round because I didn't want to see what I was losing. I stole a breath when she told me I was 14 weeks pregnant.

I was still in shock as I was led towards a different section of the clinic. Again, Mum wasn't allowed to go with me, but she gave me a hug.

'Be brave,' she whispered.

I didn't feel it. The waiting room was sparse. As I looked around my eyes fixed on the door. I wondered what would happen if I ran out and didn't stop running. Maybe if I ran no one would be able to hurt me or harm my baby. I'd find a way. I'd take care of us both and we'd be happy together – a small family unit. I'd have something to keep, someone I could call my own. The more I thought about it, the more I wanted to run from the room but I knew it was pointless. Zeb would find me; he'd hurt me and the baby. The baby would be proof of what they'd been doing to me.

I started talking to my baby. No one could hear but I knew that my unborn child could. *I'm so sorry, please forgive me. I want to keep you but I can't. If I did, everyone would know and I don't know what they'd do to me. I'd probably get into trouble. Things would be awful; we'd have no life. I've got to let you go, I hope you understand. I hope you can forgive me. I love you.*

I was still speaking silently in my head when a nurse entered the room. She handed me a blue gown and asked me to put it on. My throat constricted with fear. Right now I was pregnant but soon there'd be an empty and hollow space: my baby would be gone forever.

With a heavy heart I walked into the operating theatre.

'You'll feel a little prick in your hand, but it's just a scratch, nothing to worry about,' the anaesthetist explained.

He pushed something sharp into the back of my hand. I saw the nurse at my side and beckoned to her with my eyes. She glanced down as I opened my mouth and tried to speak.

'Please, don't do it, I've…I've changed my mi…' but the words slurred as my body shut down. My mind went into a deep sleep, taking me far away from the theatre and the clinic. Everything went black. It was too late. I'd tried to tell the nurse I didn't want to do this, that I'd changed my mind. But when I awoke, I was sore and bloodied and I felt as though I'd been butchered.

I was led to a recovery area with other women who'd just been through the same procedure. Like the other room, this was comfortable and homely with reclining chairs which seemed odd and out of place – they looked like beach chairs. But this wasn't a day out and we weren't there to relax – this was a place where they terminated pregnancies and I'd just killed my baby.

Nausea overwhelmed me and I grabbed a grey paper cup and threw up. I felt battered, as if I'd just been run over by a bus. I knew the physical pain would heal but the mental scars would remain with me forever.

I'd undergone a general anaesthetic so I had to stay at the clinic a little longer. Somehow it made me feel worse. I was still sat there when others came and went through the door. I saw all of them but I didn't make eye contact; this wasn't the place to make friends.

A taxi picked us up from the city centre and as we began the long journey home, Mum and I sat in complete silence. Neither of us knew what to say. I'd done what I'd come to do, but now all I felt was a crushing numbness.

The following day there was a knock at the front door. I heard a familiar voice – it was Dean. It was late at night but he'd come to speak to me about something. I hadn't seen him for a few days.

'I'm here because of you and the baby,' he told me. The word 'baby' stood out from the rest and knifed me straight through the heart. Dean looked awkward, standing there in the front room. Mum and Phil were in the kitchen.

'I've been thinking about us, and the baby,' he said.

My head was all jumbled. Why did he keep saying that word?

'I think we should keep it. I'll do what it takes, I'll stand by you, Katie – I want us to be together. I want to do the right thing.'

My heart sank; he didn't know.

'There is no baby,' I told him. My voice sounded hard and clinical, void of all emotion. 'I had an abortion yesterday.'

Dean physically doubled up before me. I'd done it to him – I'd caused that pain.

'Right…' was all he could muster. 'I see.'

I felt like a complete shit. Dean was a decent and honest lad. He'd come back to tell me how he'd changed his mind. Even though I'd confessed about the other men, he was prepared to stand by me. If I hadn't hit rock bottom before, I had now.

'I'm sorry,' I said as he turned to leave. I placed my hand on his shoulder. He briefly turned to look at me but his eyes were full of hurt. I hated myself more in that moment than I ever had before. I'd killed my baby; I could have said no but I'd chosen to do it. It was all my fault and now I couldn't even stand myself.

In the weeks that followed, my heart ached. I'd fallen pregnant in the most callous way but that baby had been *my* baby, no one else's – just mine. I didn't know if it was a boy or a girl but in my heart I was convinced it was a boy. He'd had no one to protect him, only me, but I hadn't and now it was too late – he was dead and gone. I hated myself for it. After the abortion my life felt totally worthless.

One day, a month after the abortion, I walked into Wadi's shop but he was nowhere to be seen. Instead, I spoke to a man who told me his name was Rafan. He worked for Wadi. I'd seen him countless times before shifting boxes in and out of the shop but, other than that, I didn't really know him. As soon as he saw me, he looked up and smiled broadly. I asked if Wadi was in but Rafan shook his head.

'No, he's out,' he replied, still grinning at me.

'But is it something I can help you with?' he said, giving me a knowing wink.

I tried not to blush. It was obvious he liked me.

THE ABORTION

With Wadi nowhere to be seen, I stood and chatted to Rafan for a while. He was very charming and I felt flattered by the attention he paid me. Rafan started to flirt. I enjoyed his company but, with no sign of Wadi, I eventually said goodbye and wandered back home.

A few days later, Lauren called over to see me so I took her to the shop. Rafan was there and he smiled when he saw us. It was obvious that Lauren fancied him but I knew what these men were like and I knew that I needed to protect her from him.

When Rafan asked us to go for a drive in his car, Lauren readily agreed. Her eyes flashed with excitement as we climbed into the back seat. Soon, we'd pulled up outside a house in a different town. Like the secret house, it looked ordinary from the outside, nestled against normal terraced properties.

Rafan poured us both a drink. Lauren giggled as we all began to laugh and joke but I felt a little nervous. Another man came downstairs and started talking to Lauren. Soon we were all drinking and smoking joints but the dope was stronger than anything I'd had before. It knocked me off-guard. The man was stroking Lauren's arm and she looked uncomfortable. Suddenly I didn't want to be there, but Rafan poured me another drink. He asked if I wanted to go and 'chill' upstairs with him. I knew what that meant and what he was after. I didn't want him to start on Lauren – I had to protect her – so I went along with him.

Lauren looked at me. Her face was hurt and confused, as though I'd betrayed her. Rafan took me to a bedroom where he started to kiss me. We smoked some more joints and I drank stuff I'd never even tried before. Eventually, the room began to spin and I covered my mouth.

'I'm going to be sick,' I gasped. I ran along the landing into the bathroom. The noise brought Lauren and the man running upstairs. I vomited a bright green liquid in the toilet bowl. Rafan's mate tapped me on the back; it made my flesh crawl.

'Leave me alone,' I hissed at him.

I cleaned myself up but I felt wretched. I stumbled downstairs but Rafan followed and started pawing my body, offering me more joints and alcohol.

'Leave her alone!' It was Lauren's voice. 'Can't you see she's not well?'

But he wasn't listening.

'Come upstairs,' he said, dragging me to my feet. Limply, I staggered behind him.

We had sex and eventually returned downstairs to Lauren and the strange man in the front room. But Lauren wouldn't look at me. I could tell she hated me for having sex with Rafan – the man she fancied. I couldn't explain it to her but I knew what he wanted and how he wouldn't stop until he'd got his own way. My life was already ruined; I wouldn't let him ruin hers too.

Afterwards, Lauren barely spoke to me. She felt I'd betrayed her but I knew all I'd done was protect her.

In the weeks that followed, I began to bleed in between periods. Rafan hadn't used any protection and for a moment, I was gripped with fear that I might be pregnant again. I needed to know one way or another so I travelled to a GUM clinic in a hospital on the other side of town. I lied and told them I'd had unprotected sex with my boyfriend.

'I'm worried I could be pregnant,' I confessed.

Thankfully, I wasn't but further tests revealed something else: I had Chlamydia. It seems I had saved Lauren in more ways than one.

THE ABORTION

I was given a two-week course of antibiotics but I almost didn't care. Having a sexually transmitted infection wasn't as bad as having an abortion. Nothing else could hurt me as much as that had.

It was suggested I have a coil fitted to prevent further pregnancies. I readily agreed. Before the baby, it hadn't occurred to me that I might actually get pregnant. It sounds stupid and naive but somehow I thought I was too young. Following the abortion, I was determined I wouldn't get caught out again.

Rafan continued to text me and we met again a few weeks later. This time he took me to another house. Unlike the other, this one had furniture. We went upstairs into a pink bedroom. I could tell it was a little girl's room, yet despite that, we still had unprotected sex on the single bed.

This time I stayed overnight – I lied and told Mum I was staying at Lauren's. The following morning when I woke up, Rafan was gone. I got dressed and made my way out onto the landing. Moments later, another Asian man came out of a second bedroom. He studied me for a moment and spoke.

'I'm just about to have a shower but you must wait for me,' he said, grabbing my arm. 'We can have fun – we can chill together.'

By now, of course, I knew what 'chill' meant – it was a code word for sex.

'Okay,' I smiled. The man leered back at me and used his other hand to stroke my face.

'I'll be just here,' I told him, pointing back at the bedroom.

He grinned and headed into the bathroom.

As soon as I heard the shower click on, I fled downstairs and out of the house. I didn't stop running until I reached my front door. Only then did I feel safe.

I knew I'd been stupid to have unprotected sex with Rafan again so I returned to the GUM clinic, where they told me I'd contracted Chlamydia for a second time. I should have felt disgusted; I'd known Rafan had given it to me in the first place and now he'd done it again. But I was past caring – all my emotions had been blunted by the abortion. I was in meltdown and nothing or no one could stop me. I continued this way, in my spiral of self-destruction, over the next few weeks.

Then another man who worked at Wadi's shop started talking to me. His name was Isam. He asked for my mobile number so I gave it to him. He gave me beer and took me to the countryside. Once, he drove me and Lauren there and we saw Rafan drive past in his car, but he didn't see us.

Isam parked up and pushed a coat up against the windows. He told Lauren to get in the front and draped a blanket across the front seats so she couldn't see. Then he told me to get on the back seat, where he had sex with me. He even turned up the radio so it was loud enough to cover the noises he made.

Lauren never said much to me after that – I think she formed her own opinion of me and what I'd become. I couldn't tell her I was only doing it to stop them from doing it to her; she wouldn't understand.

Still, I felt dirty. My GP prescribed more tablets to get rid of the sexually transmitted infection but the pills couldn't clean me inside. I'd always be scarred where my baby had been ripped from my body.

Wadi later found out about Isam and sacked him from the shop. After that, I never saw Isam again.

A female counsellor at the new school noticed my mood swings and erratic behaviour and made it clear she wanted to speak to me. She spoke to us all individually once a week anyway to see if she could help with problems at home but I never told her a thing. However, despite my loathing for school, I actually liked this woman. Her name was Rebecca.

One Friday, Rebecca called me into her room.

'Is everything alright, Katie?' she asked.

I nodded numbly, but everything was far from alright. Zeb had been on the phone chastising me for not having answered his calls. I told him that I'd been ill, but he wasn't interested. I didn't mention the baby – I knew it would just make him worse.

'I'm fine,' I answered. I told her what she wanted to hear.

'And at home? How are things at home?' she said, pressing me a little further.

'Okay, I suppose.' I shrugged my shoulders.

Rebecca was friendly and asked me if there was anything else I'd like to talk about. I told her there wasn't, but she kept on at me. I wondered if she could read it on my face. Did she suspect something? I knew it was madness. She didn't have a clue; only I knew the real truth.

'If there's anything, *anything* you ever need to talk to me about, then I'm always here. You can tell me anything, Katie. It's all confidential, just between the two of us.'

I nodded for a second time and my eyes darted over towards the door. I couldn't wait to get out of there before I blurted something out and gave the game away.

'Well,' Rebecca said, putting her hands on her knees, 'I guess we're all done here.'

I jumped to my feet and almost bolted for the door.

'But Katie,' she called, 'anytime you need to speak to me, the door,' she said, pointing to it, 'is *always* open.'

I smiled and turned back. Grabbing the door handle I

pushed it down and stepped back into cool corridor and let out a sigh of relief.

The usual call from Zeb followed a day later.

'Where have you been?' he snapped. 'I've been texting but you've not answered any of my texts.'

'Sorry,' I mumbled. I didn't mean it.

I saw Zeb that day and a few more times after that but by now I hated him. He'd made everything in my life rotten. I'd lost everything because of him and the others. I'd lost my childhood, my innocence, even my baby. At first I'd told myself he loved me, but he didn't: you didn't make someone you love have sex with complete strangers. It wasn't just odd, it was seedy and evil. He was evil.

I decided something had to give. One day I'd tell someone all about the secret house, about the Asian men. I'd come clean. But who would I tell and when? The answer came much sooner than I could ever have anticipated.

CHAPTER 19

ZEB'S PLAN

'Katie, is that you?' It was Zeb, and he sounded edgy and urgent.

'Yes,' I replied, my flesh crawling at the sound of his voice.

'I need to meet you today – I'll pick you up, usual place.'

'Err…I can't,' I lied. 'I'm busy.'

'This is important – I need to speak to you about something. Be there. 4pm, and DON'T be late!' he warned.

I sat in school watching the clock above the teacher's head. Soon it would be time to go home, but not to the safety of Mum and Phil. Tonight I'd walk into the arms of a monster. Part of me was curious – I wondered what he wanted to speak to me about. What was so important that it couldn't wait? Maybe it was something good. Whatever it was, I wouldn't know unless I met him.

Zeb was in the front of Aban's car in the alleyway as I approached. He smiled as soon as he saw me; he was in a good mood.

'Katie,' he said, holding out his arms as if greeting an old friend, 'get in, get in!'

But his happy mood set me on edge. I knew him well and

when he was like this it made me nervous because I couldn't second-guess what was coming next.

'What did you want to speak to me about?' I asked.

'Oh, *that*? Never mind, have a drag on this,' he said, handing me a spliff.

I inhaled the smoke and felt my tense body relax.

'Let's go to the house, we can talk there,' he said, waving his hand at Aban in the driver's seat.

Aban turned the key in the ignition and off we set towards the secret house. Once inside, Zeb handed me a large vodka and Coke.

'Drink it,' he urged. 'It'll help you relax.'

I did as he said and let the warm alcohol slide down the back of my throat.

'Thirsty?' he laughed, as he poured me another.

Zeb took me in his arms and cuddled me, something he rarely did. I felt my body stiffen underneath his touch. Something wasn't right, I just knew it. He was in an unnaturally good mood. Something was coming.

We smoked spliff after spliff and I drank the other large vodka and Coke, only this time I noticed there was more vodka than Coke in it.

'Have you ever tried the other coke?' Zeb said. He was staring at me, as if for the first time.

'What, cocaine?' I replied.

'Yep.' He nodded and started to laugh.

I told him I hadn't. I was fifteen years old, and alcohol and cannabis were the only drugs I'd ever tried. Cocaine was for junkies and I wasn't one of them.

'Listen, Katie,' he said, putting his drink down on the coffee table. 'I need you to do something for me.'

I looked at him. This was it; this was what he'd brought me here to tell me.

'I need you to have sex with other men,' he said bluntly.

The words made me choke on my drink and I started to cough. What did he think I'd been doing in this house? I'd been having sex with his friends all this time. But he wasn't finished.

'What do you mean?' I asked, panic rising inside me.

'I want you to have sex for money,' he explained. 'I want you to have sex with strangers for money.'

I was so shocked that I dropped my glass back down on the table. The brown liquid rose up and splashed over the edge. I stared at the puddle.

'For *money*?' I repeated.

'Uh huh,' Zeb grunted as he took another drag on his spliff, 'Yep.'

He blew a cloud of smoke out from his mouth. 'It'll be fine because we'll split the money between us. You and me – it'd be like a business arrangement.'

I shook my head vehemently.

'No way! No way, Zeb!' I said, rising to my feet.

'Katie, relax, sit down! You do me favours here anyway – the only difference is you'll get paid for it now. And I'll give you cocaine, as much as you want. You can sniff it up your nose – it'll make you feel good. It'll make you feel sexy,' he leered.

My stomach churned as I watched the word 'sexy' dance on his lips. I felt sick. I knew exactly what he meant – Zeb wanted to turn me into a prostitute. He'd get me hooked on cocaine so I'd rely on him to feed my habit. Things were bad enough but now it seemed he had my whole future mapped out: I'd be a prostitute and he'd be my pimp.

'We'd have money – lots of it,' he explained, excitement rising in his voice.

'Think what you could do with all that money. You wouldn't have to worry, you could live here with me – I'll look after you. I'll take care of you forever.'

His eyes shone the more he spoke. I couldn't believe it – he was serious.

Zeb looked over, searching my face for an answer, but I didn't give one.

'Well?' he snapped, 'what do you think?'

I knew what I thought but I was too frightened to say.

'What if I don't like the men, what if they're old and ugly? I wouldn't have to have sex with them if I didn't want to, would I?'

Zeb's face clouded over and he became angry.

'Of course you would, you silly bitch! You won't be able to refuse. If they pay you'll have to do it because you'll be providing a service. It's a business for Christ's sake – it'll make you rich!'

But I didn't want to be rich – I wanted to be safe. I wanted Zeb out of my life for good, but all I could think was that I needed to get out of there in one piece.

'Err…I'll think about it,' I promised. I knew I'd have to play along just to keep him happy. If I said no, God only knows what he'd do to me.

I prayed my voice sounded convincing enough.

'Good, good,' Zeb said. 'Now finish your drink and Aban will take you home.'

I got straight to my feet – I didn't need telling twice.

'But Katie…' Zeb called as I neared the front door. My heart thudded violently inside my chest.

'I'll call you tomorrow, okay? Don't take too long to think about it. It's a good offer – it will make us both rich!'

I smiled tightly back at him but my entire body felt rigid with fear. Calmly, I closed the door, walked out into the street and climbed into the back of Aban's car.

'Take me home, please,' I begged.

Aban turned the key in the ignition and the car fired into life. As the countryside whizzed by, I knew it was time: I had to tell someone. It was now or never.

CHAPTER 20

TELLING SOMEONE

That evening I couldn't sleep. I had nightmares and they were full of Zeb: he was coming for me and there was no escape.

I dreamt I was on a fairground helter-skelter but someone was chasing me with a knife. I was certain it was Zeb. I slid down the ride but became stuck halfway. The slide began to fill with water so I had to get off. I jumped to the ground but there were three men waiting for me. I couldn't see their faces but I recognised one voice – Zeb's. Two men pinned me down whilst Zeb tried to suffocate me using a plastic bag.

The next morning, I was so traumatised both my pyjamas and bed were sodden with sweat. I couldn't eat breakfast because I felt sick and all churned up inside. Instead I grabbed my bag and raced to school; I had to tell someone about Zeb before he trapped me for good. I knew exactly what to do and who I should tell – Rebecca. She was the school counsellor; she'd know what to do.

I ran to school and went straight to the office but Rebecca was nowhere to be seen. A teacher passed.

'Is Rebecca in today?' I asked, a little breathless.

'I think so, maybe this afternoon?' the teacher replied.

My body shrank at the news. I was ready to tell her now but she wasn't there. Inside I was panicking because I knew that I had to speak to her before Zeb got to me. I didn't realise but the stress and worry showed on my face.

'Is everything alright, Katie?' the teacher asked.

'Yes,' I mumbled.

I made an excuse, hitched up my bag and headed off into the classroom. I didn't tell her because I didn't trust her. The only person I could tell was Rebecca. I could tell her anything, she'd said so. She wouldn't tell anyone else, either – it was all confidential. Rebecca would know what to do; she'd know how to make this stop.

I knew I was out of my depth with Zeb. The situation had changed overnight. He had a plan and he wanted me to be part of it but I didn't want to be, not anymore.

I prayed Rebecca would arrive before Zeb rang.

A few hours later I was in the corridor when I heard someone call my name: it was Rebecca.

'I heard you were looking for me,' she smiled. 'I'm here now – do you want to come through to the office?'

I was relieved, but as I followed her I had second thoughts. I wondered if this was a good idea after all – what if she judged me? What if she thought I was a slag? Then I thought about Zeb – how he'd said he was my boyfriend. What if she thought I was just some stupid kid who couldn't handle a relationship? By the time we sat down and closed the door, I was lost for words.

'Well?' she said softly, trying to prompt me. 'Is there something you'd like to tell me? Is there something troubling you?'

I looked over at her. Rebecca was dressed in trendy jeans and a cool top. She was obviously older than me but she still looked young and nothing at all like a teacher or a counsellor. She'd understand. She *had* to – I had no one else I could turn to.

'You said everything I tell you is confidential?' I began nervously.

'Absolutely,' she replied. 'Everything you tell me in here is confidential. You can tell me anything – nothing will shock me.'

I thought for a moment. Maybe it wasn't so shocking at all. Maybe it was totally normal and really quite boring. Maybe I'd just built it up inside my head into something it wasn't. Rebecca would just know how to stop Zeb's plan – I could handle everything else. I didn't want to become Zeb's prostitute, that's all. My life wasn't perfect but I could live with the rest.

'There is a man,' I told her, my voice quiet and a little shaky to begin with. 'I've never told anyone this before but he takes me to a house. It's in the next town…'

I stopped mid-sentence. I'd said it – I'd told her about the secret house. Zeb would kill me if he ever found out.

'What house, Katie? Is it his house?'

'Yes, sort of,' I guessed. 'Other men go there too but I think he owns it.'

'And this man,' she said, leaning forward, 'what does he take you to this house for? What do you do when you get there?'

My hands knotted together nervously in my lap and I glanced downwards. I couldn't look at her because I felt too ashamed.

'We have sex,' I replied, my voice barely a whisper.

'You and this man have sex in this house. Where is this house, Katie? You must tell me. And how old is this man?'

'He's older than me – I think he's married – but he said I can't tell anyone about the house because it's a secret house.'

Rebecca's eyes widened. She looked shocked but she tried to hide it.

'But it's normal,' I said, beginning to panic. 'It's okay because he takes care of me.'

Rebecca nodded but it was obvious she didn't agree.

'No, really, it's fine because he's my boyfriend. We just smoke a few spliffs and have a drink,' I said, suddenly starting to backtrack. I wondered if I was doing the right thing.

'But Katie,' Rebecca said, leaning further forwards towards me in her chair. 'Can't you see it's *not* normal? He's older than you. You are fifteen years old. You're underage – you shouldn't be having sex.'

I knew she'd mention the age thing. For a moment I even wondered if I was in trouble, but I could tell from the look on her face I wasn't. I opened my mouth and inhaled a deep breath to calm my nerves. I wasn't finished yet.

'It's not just him,' I sighed. I couldn't look at her. 'There are other men and they're all Asian – I have sex with them all.'

Rebecca gasped so loud it made me look up.

'But it's okay…' I reasoned. 'It's normal because they love me.'

She shook her head in horror as I said the words.

'No, it's not normal, Katie, can't you see that? It just isn't. These men, this man, they're abusing you – you're still a child.'

Abuse. The word came out of nowhere and hit me. I'd never thought of it like that before. I was still a child and these were grown men, but they didn't care how old I was when they had sex with me. She was right, it *was* abuse – it was child abuse and I was the victim.

My voice cracked with emotion – there was so much more to tell.

'I got pregnant and had to have an abortion. It was horrible.' I said breaking down. 'I wanted to keep the baby,' I sobbed. 'It was the only good thing to have come out of all of this but everyone talked me out of it. Mum knows about the baby…'

I looked up because I realised how much I'd said.

'But she doesn't know about the men – *please* don't tell her, don't tell Mum!' I begged.

Once I began, the rest of my tears came thick and fast. Rebecca leaned over and grabbed a box of tissues, which she handed to me. I nodded gratefully.

'Tell me about the man,' she said softly, 'What else does he make you do?'

'Zeb?' I asked. 'He's my boyfriend but he makes me have sex with other men in the house. I'm frightened of him but I have to do as he tells me otherwise he says he'll rape Mum and make me watch.'

Rebecca couldn't help it. She gasped with horror and flopped back into her chair.

'He's *threatened* you?'

'No…Yes…I don't know…' I wept. My head was buzzing. It felt all tangled up inside, confused and messy.

'Have you told anyone else about this Zeb?' she asked.

'No, only you. But there's something else; something I haven't told you.'

Rebecca leaned forward and held my hand in hers. 'Go on,' she urged.

'He wants me to have sex with more men – strangers. He says he's going to charge them for sex but he'll split the money with me. He says we'll be rich. But I don't want to be rich, Rebecca – I just want to be normal.'

My voice faded as more tears came. Rebecca soothed me but I could tell she was horrified and was still trying to process everything I'd just told her.

'You've done the right thing coming to see me,' she finally said. 'And I'm going to help you, Katie.'

It was all I needed to hear. Her words eased the pain I felt inside. Soon I'd told her everything.

'He says he's going to give me cocaine – he wants me to rely on him. But I don't want to be a prostitute and I don't want to take cocaine. I'm frightened,' I admitted. 'He's going to ring me to see what my answer is. What am I going to tell him?' I added, my voice high with panic.

'You ignore his calls,' Rebecca insisted, her eyes fixed firmly on mine, 'You don't answer any of his calls from now on, Katie. Promise me.'

I looked at her.

'Promise.'

'Good girl,' she said.

For the first time in years I felt as though the big black cloud hanging above my head had cleared. Things had become clearer. I was glad I'd come to see Rebecca, glad that I'd finally found the courage to tell someone.

She sat and listened as I told her how Zeb had threatened me countless times.

'He'd said no one would ever believe me – he said everyone would think I was a slapper.'

'He's trying to control you,' she told me.

'You don't think I'm a slag, do you?' I asked.

'Of course not,' she replied. 'You're the victim in all this, Katie. You're a child – you've done nothing wrong. This man has taken advantage of you and he must be stopped.'

'*Stopped*?' I gasped. The word stuck in my throat.

I didn't want her to stop Zeb because to do that I knew she'd have to speak to him, then he'd know I'd told her everything, then he'd rape Mum and hurt me.

'But he *can't* know I've told you!' I said, panic rising in my voice.

'Katie, if we don't stop him now he'll do this to another girl. He'll ruin another young life. You don't want that to happen, do you?'

I shook my head. Rebecca was right.

'Listen,' she said, getting up from her chair. 'I need to tell Adrian about this.'

I began to cry once more. I didn't want Adrian to know – he was the centre manager and Rebecca's boss.

'But you said it was confidential!' I cried. 'You said it was between you and me!'

I was panicking now. This was really happening. My secret was out and soon everyone would know.

But Rebecca was adamant.

'Katie, I have a duty of care to you and all the other kids here. I have to report this – it's what they call "guilty knowledge". I can't just ignore it. If I did, I wouldn't be doing my job properly.'

'But you can't, *please*…' I begged.

'Katie, this man needs to be stopped before he hurts anyone else. This is the only way to do it. Trust me.'

I pleaded with Rebecca not to tell Adrian but she wouldn't

listen. I'd trusted her but now I felt she'd lied to me. Once Adrian knew, he'd tell Mum, Dad, even Phil.

Then I remembered and my stomach lurched.

Oh God, I thought, *Zeb is going to kill me!*

CHAPTER 21

THE INVESTIGATION

The abuse with Zeb and his circle of friends had gone on for almost two years but now it was no longer my secret to keep. I thought if I continued to keep him happy then he wouldn't rape Mum. I believed that by having sex with him, I was protecting her. But I was wrong. I came to realise that it wouldn't make any difference. Zeb never had any intention of raping Mum; all he'd ever wanted to do was turn me into a prostitute. Everything that had happened had been about him and always had been. Rebecca helped me see things clearly for the first time.

This was about control, greed and money. Zeb had raped and abused me for so long I'd become numb, almost used to it. I even believed him when he said that I didn't matter. I truly believed I was there to be used, abused and thrown away. But Rebecca made me realise I was worth more than that; I could fight Zeb and I was allowed to say no. More importantly, I had the power to stop him from hurting others.

Rebecca left the room to speak to Adrian. Fear gripped me when I imagined Zeb's face. Suddenly I doubted that I was strong enough to see this through. For a fleeting moment I thought about running out to the street outside. I'd run along roads and streets until I couldn't run anymore. But then I remembered Donna – the girl at school. She'd spent her life running away from her problems but they always followed her from one school to the next. I didn't want to be like her, I didn't want to spend the rest of my life running. Now it was time to stop.

Moments later, Rebecca came back into the room.

'Adrian has called the police and they want me to go and speak to them.'

I gulped. Police? I thought of the station; it was right next door to the school unit.

'I'm not going,' I said, beginning to panic again.

'You don't have to, Katie, I'll tell them everything,' she explained.

'But they'll say it's my fault – I'll get into trouble,' I fretted.

'Katie,' Rebecca reassured me. 'None of this is your fault. You are a child, you've done nothing wrong.'

I wanted to believe her but part of me was terrified about what I'd just done. I knew Zeb would kill me when he found out.

Rebecca grabbed her bag, left the room and went to the police station. The longer I sat alone, the more I cringed. She'd be there right now, talking about me. I hated the idea of strangers knowing all about my sex life. What would they think of me? Zeb was right; they'd think I was a slapper.

But more than that, I was terrified of what Zeb, Wadi and Tali would do to me when the police turned up on their doorsteps.

Suddenly, the urge to feel safe and protected overwhelmed me. I grabbed my things, left the room and ran to the street outside. I didn't stop running until I'd made it home.

I glanced down at my watch – it was 3pm. I'd told Rebecca over two hours ago. It wouldn't be long before the police arrived.

Mum was in the kitchen cooking as I closed the front door.

'Katie, is that you?' she called.

For a second my heart froze – did she know?

'Good day?' she asked, popping her head round the doorway to greet me. It was clear she didn't.

'Yeah,' I mumbled. I walked into the front room and sank down onto the sofa. It faced the window. I needed to see – I needed to be prepared. I thought that maybe I could deny everything. The police would ask and I'd tell them I'd made it up. I'd be in trouble but not as much as I would be if this got out. But no, I told myself, there'd been enough lies. Now was time for truth.

My heart was pounding. I put a hand to my chest to steady it but it did no good. It was just two weeks before my sixteenth birthday; what if I got into trouble with the police for having underage sex? What if Zeb blamed me and said I was a prostitute? What if they believed him and not me? He was clever and good at manipulating people. I fretted as all these thoughts raced through my mind. What if he convinced the police it was my fault – that I was just a silly little slag?

My mind raced with different scenarios. I was replaying all the possibilities in my head when I noticed a dark car pull up outside. A man and woman got out but they didn't look like police officers – they were dressed in ordinary clothes. I heard a knock at the front door but I remained seated, my senses on full alert. Mum went to the door and answered it and I heard someone say my name.

'Can we come in?' a woman asked.

'What's this about?' Mum started to say, but she was interrupted. 'Can we speak to Katie, please, is she in?'

I stepped out into the hallway and as I did so all three turned to look at me. I felt my face flush.

'Katie?' the woman asked.

I looked over at her. She was smartly dressed – I guessed she must be a plain-clothes police officer. I nodded in acknowledgement. I knew why they were there but Mum was baffled. Her eyes flitted between us.

'Can someone please tell me what on earth is going on?' she said, her voice tense and nervous.

'Shall we?' the man said, gesturing towards the front room.

Once inside, he asked us to take a seat but Mum refused. She was spiky and defensive because she knew they were police officers and she thought I'd done something awful.

'If you've done anything…' she began, but the woman stopped her.

'My name is Angela and I'm a female detective,' she said, looking over at me rather than at Mum. 'We want to speak to Katie because there's a group of Asian men and we believe they've been hurting your daughter.'

My eyes glanced down at the carpet and I prayed that the ground would open up and swallow me whole. Mum looked at me and then back at Angela. She still didn't understand.

'These Asian men…' Angela continued, '…we believe they've been having sex with your daughter.'

My face burned. Right then, I wanted to be anywhere else. I couldn't look up, but I didn't need to – I could imagine the horror on Mum's face. Her defensive body language suddenly disintegrated as she flopped down onto the arm of the chair. The words had just knocked the stuffing clean out of her.

The silence in the room was deafening. I waited for them to say something to me. I waited for the police to arrest me for having sex at just fifteen years old. But they didn't.

'I can't believe it,' Mum finally said.

'Katie? *My* Katie? Are you sure?'

I looked up and saw Angela nod her head.

'We need to speak to your daughter because we need to know what she can tell us. Katie, would that be alright? Can you tell us what's been happening to you?'

I gulped as my body began to tremble. There was no going back; this was it and I was simply terrified.

'I…I *can't*,' I stammered. 'I can't tell you because if I do, they'll kill me!'

All the pent-up emotion came spilling out and I began to cry. Deep sobs rose up from within me as my body shook with fear.

I didn't want to tell them what I'd been doing, not in front of Mum. I didn't want to tell them because I was certain that if I did, Zeb would kill me.

'They know where I live. I can't tell you. I can't because if I do, he'll kill me.'

The female detective nodded and promised she wouldn't let anyone harm me.

'Who is it, Katie? Who is it you're frightened of?' she asked. 'You need to tell us; if you don't, we can't help you.'

I realised it was finally time. My secret was out and now it was time to stop running. Time to stop living in fear.

'They gave me drink – alcohol, and they gave me joints to

249

STOLEN GIRL

smoke. But it's okay,' I insisted. 'It's okay because it's normal. They're my boyfriends – they said they'd look after me…' But as I heard my own voice I knew how ridiculous this now sounded.

Mum clasped her hand over her mouth in horror. The more she heard, the more she wept.

Slowly, I told them everything. But the more I revealed, the more I realised how very little I actually knew about these men. Yet Zeb and the others knew everything about me. Everything. I'd been abused for almost three years. It started with Sam and then the others but they were all as bad as one another. They were all to blame but I was frightened – scared of what they'd do to me.

'But I can't tell you who they are or where they're from,' I said, beginning to panic again. It was a lie. I knew where to find them all, but I also knew that if I led the police to their doors, I'd be as good as dead.

The police didn't believe me. They knew that I knew more than I was letting on.

'But if I tell you their names then I'm going to die!' I wailed.

Thankfully, the detectives agreed to leave me alone and give me more time. They realised they wouldn't get much more out of me that afternoon. They left, but told me they'd return the following morning.

After they'd left Mum could barely look at me. It was as though I'd become a stranger to her. I just wanted her to wrap her arms around me and tell me everything would be okay but she didn't. Instead, she sat numb and silent in a corner of the room.

Zeb never rang me again. I knew then it was over.

The following day the police came back. They asked me more and more until slowly the whole story unravelled.

'Katie, none of this is your fault,' Angela reassured me. 'We're here to stop these men from doing this and from hurting anyone else.'

But somewhere in the back of my mind, I still believed I was somehow to blame. I'd been a willing party. I believed they were still my boyfriends.

Angela shook her head when I said it.

'If they're your boyfriends then why were they hiding you away? Why did Zeb insist you mustn't tell anyone about him or the house?'

'But they love me, they care about me…' I said, in a bout of misplaced loyalty.

'If they care about you, why would they give you drugs and alcohol? You're still a child; they did that so they could abuse you. You were vulnerable and they took advantage,' Angela insisted.

The fog in my mind cleared. Angela was right, just as Rebecca had been – none of this was my fault.

A few weeks later, I celebrated my sixteenth birthday but with the ongoing police investigation, there was little to be joyful about. Instead the police came to see me at home with a camera. Another female police officer asked me questions but Angela and Rebecca, the counsellor I'd told at school, were there too. Their support helped me greatly.

I answered each and every question as honestly as I could. Thankfully, Mum, Phil and Andrew left the house to give me more privacy.

Mum rang my dad to tell him and, as expected, he was really supportive, although I still wasn't sure how much he actually knew.

'I don't care, Katie,' he said, wrapping his arms around

me protectively. 'I'm always here for you whenever you need me.'

The more I told the police about the abuse, the angrier I became. The rage boiled up inside me and came spilling out. To control it and to bring some sort of order back into my life, I upped the self-harm. Now I was harming myself most nights. Whenever the crimson blood stripe appeared across my wrist I'd immediately feel better and more at peace. Self-harm was the only thing I had control over now, the rest of my life was in freefall.

Andrew didn't really understand at the beginning and blamed me for all the tension in the house. He said he felt ashamed of me.

'It's all your fault!' he screamed one day. Mum was crying again in the kitchen.

'You got involved with these men – you're nothing but a dirty slag!'

I hated him for saying it, but then I hated myself even more. How could I have been so stupid?

Phil tried his best to keep out of any arguments. The strain was taking its toll on each and every one of us and slowly, it was destroying us all.

'Why didn't you tell me or someone else?' Mum sobbed one night.

'I didn't know how to. You were so wrapped up in your new life that there was no room for me.'

Mum held her hand against her chest as if I'd just stabbed her through the heart. In many ways I had – with words. But part of me wanted to hurt her. I was angry – angry that she hadn't protected me and angry she hadn't noticed something was wrong. But the reality was, it wasn't her fault. It wasn't even mine. It was the bastards who'd done this to me. They'd ruined my life and taken everything from me but now they were going to pay.

The police recorded everything I said on tape. Dozens of hours of interviews were burned onto eight DVDs. They would be evidence. Now they had everything, it was time to raid the secret house.

CHAPTER 22

BACK TO THE SECRET HOUSE

'Just show us in your own time,' the officer said gently. I didn't know the name of the road, but I knew my way to the secret house like the back of my hand.

'Turn left down here,' I told him, as the unmarked car indicated and made its way down the familiar old street.

'It's just up here – the one with the white door.'

As the car drew close, fear overwhelmed me and I ducked down and curled myself up on the back seat. There was a detective sitting right beside me but I was frightened – I couldn't believe I was actually doing this.

My fingerprints and DNA had been taken at the time of the interviews. When Angela stuck something inside my mouth, I asked her what it was for.

'It's so we can tell if you've been inside the house.'

Afterwards, they'd driven me past so I could point out the secret house – only it wasn't a secret anymore. We didn't stop or park up, we just drove straight past. The police didn't want to do anything that might have drawn attention.

Being so close again brought all the old fears rushing back.

'What if they hurt me? Zeb knows where I live – he might come to get me,' I sobbed in a state of panic.

But Angela reassured me.

'He won't. You don't have to be frightened anymore.'

The tears streamed down my face as I realised what a fool I'd been to think that Zeb had ever loved me. He'd just used me. But I'd always been frightened, too scared to tell anyone about him or the secret house. Now, I hated myself for keeping quiet for so long. If only I'd spoken out sooner. The guilt weighed heavy in my heart. I felt angry with myself but I knew I was doing the right thing. Angela cleared her throat and looked at me.

'We've had another girl come forward – she was just twelve years old when the abuse started.'

I felt sick.

'*Twelve*?' I repeated.

'Yes,' said Angela. 'She knew the men by different names. However, like you, she pointed out exactly the same house.'

The girl had read about the men's arrests in the local paper and had telephoned the police to tell them. But she was young and far too frightened to testify against Zeb and the others. I understood her pain. There were probably others out there but they were all too scared to come forward and say what had really happened inside that horrible house.

The investigation rumbled on and the months passed by slowly so, to try and make some kind of sense of the pain and anger I held inside, I kept a diary. The family liaison officer suggested it – she thought it might help me to write things down. It did.

The police had interviewed each man. Some denied knowing me, but thankfully the police obtained their mobile phone records, which proved otherwise. The depths these bastards would plunge to and the lies they would tell in order to save their own necks were unbelievable.

The more the investigation rumbled on, the more I feared that someone would come to get me; a friend or relative of Zeb's. I lived with the fear daily.

Finally, after almost two painstaking years, the police told me that six men had been charged, each one accused of using me for sex. There were also different charges of rape and a catalogue of sexual offences – 38 in total.

Unfortunately, police were unable to trace some of the men who'd abused me at the secret house – Hakim, Habis and Jad – all friends of Zeb's. The police believe as soon as they heard of Zeb's arrest, the men had fled to Pakistan. There were the others too – the faceless unnamed men in the front room. The ones I believed had gang-raped me. However, the police had little hope of finding them because I didn't even know their names and could barely remember what they looked like. They were as guilty as Zeb and the others but they had simply vanished off the face of the earth, it seemed.

CHAPTER 23

THE DIARY

A s I waited for the day to come for the men to enter their pleas, my anger spilled out into words in my diary. The more I wrote, the more my anger and frustration bubbled up and rose to the surface. Writing was my therapy; the words helped me make sense of it all.

29th April: *I went to the coast with Dad today. I laughed quite a lot when we were there but I suppose it's all a front. I was supposed to have a good time and my dad thought I was but I did it for him, to stop him worrying. All I could think about was what I've got to go through with the trial.*

30th April: *I didn't do much today, just moped around in my dressing gown. I'm 16, but I feel as if my life is over. I have no future. There's nothing to celebrate.*

2nd May: *I feel depressed, angry, hurt and frustrated. I don't want to be here anymore.*

4th May: *I'm scared when it comes to the trial, I won't be able to do it. I'm terrified of going to court. The only good thing is I've been spending a lot of time with Dad again. He cares for me and loves me very much. He keeps telling me this.*

5th May: *I didn't do anything today. I got up at 4.20pm. I didn't even have a shower. My bedroom is a tip, the floor is a mess and I haven't made my bed. My desk is a state and the floor too. My whole life is a mess. I feel blank and empty. Things are hitting me properly – this is really happening.*

6th May: *Got up at 2.15pm and made dinner. I shouldn't have to tell people I'm depressed, they should notice and see what a mess I am. But then, why should they? I've always been alone through this. Although I feel down, I'm determined to see this through.*

13th May: *Time is flying by. Usually, when I'm waiting for something, time goes slow. The closer the court hearing gets, the more scared I become.*

14th May: *I'm just waiting until next month when the bastards plead. I don't think they'll plead guilty – they haven't got the guts. They're all cowards. I hope they rot in hell.*

24th May: *I had such a weird dream last night. I woke up and spotted an enormous spider on my wall. It was huge, the kind you see in horror movies. I screamed, got up and switched the light on but there was nothing there. There never had been. My mind is playing tricks on me, maybe it's fear?*

27th May: *Went to sleep at midday, woke up at 7.30pm. My sleeping pattern is so messed up.*

THE DIARY

28th May: *My body is tired and I feel drained. I'm physically and mentally run down all the time. I can't stand anyone talking to me. I get easily irritated. I just want to be alone.*

3rd June: *They enter their pleas a week today. I want it to pass fast so I know what they plead.*

5th June: *The police liaison officer called me today. She says I might be able to go to court to hear them enter their pleas. She's calling tomorrow.*

6th June: *She called back. They've advised me not to go even though the court is open to the public. Legally I'm allowed, but as a witness and the victim, it's awkward. She promised to call me to let me know what they plead but I think I'll hear it on the radio before she tells me. I fell asleep but woke up crying. I'm frightened they'll come to hurt me.*

8th June: *They'll plead in two days' time. I had an argument with the lady from victim support — I can't be arsed with her. My feelings are all over the place. I'm fed up of waiting.*

9th June: *Tomorrow's the day. I've waited so long for this. I just want to know. Either way, it's going to be hard for me.*

10th June: *They went to court but they didn't plead. Their lawyers asked for more time to look at evidence. They have to go back in a month and then they'll have to enter a plea — all of them.*

11th June: *I'm fed up and utterly depressed. I've been fighting for justice for over two years now, yet I'm still waiting. How much longer? A year? Two more years?*

16th June: *I cried today, I don't even know why. I guess I've tried to put the court stuff to the back of my mind but it's still there. I feel totally let down by the legal system. I'm counting the days down.*

17th June: *I want to die. I don't know where I'm going to end up but I've got a feeling it's not going to be a very good place.*

20th June: *I'm on go-slow with everything and it worries me. I can't look after myself. I'm scared of the future. I can't imagine myself all alone.*

25th June: *I have to go for an assessment tomorrow. I'm going to be asked questions on how I feel about court and the trial. The doctor/psychiatrist has to report back to the Crown Prosecution Service to say whether she thinks I'll be able to handle court or not.*

26th June: *The psychiatrist was really nice. I told her everything, that I feel suicidal all the time. She has diagnosed me with Post Traumatic Stress Disorder (PTSD). It's treatable but I can't have therapy until after the trial.*

1st July: *I told Dad about the PTSD. He was upset and offered to take me out for the day. But taking me out isn't going to take away the disorder, only therapy can do that and I'm not putting years of my life into therapy for what someone else has done to me. It's been two years and two months now waiting for justice. I've had enough.*

3rd July: *The depression is getting worse, I can feel it.*

4th July: *I got a step-by-step DVD about going to court and a leaflet.*

There was a booklet about being a witness and a form that I have to fill in and return. I'm scared.

6th July: *Dad helped me fill in the form. It all seems so certain now. I'm frightened that by going, it's going to ruin things for the rest of my life. I don't want to live.*

10th July: *I cut myself again today. The scars on my arm are deep.*

11th July: *I told the psychiatrist about my self-harming and showed her my scars.*

18th July: *I'm mentally ill. I have no control over anything. They go to court next week. I can't bear it to be delayed again.*

27th July: *They all pleaded not guilty. I knew it. They raped me for almost two years and put me through hell yet they have the nerve to stand in court and say 'not guilty'. I met my support worker, she's called Karen and she's really nice. She bought me a writing pad and a pink box to put it all in. I'm going to start a journal. I'm going to write poems and my thoughts and fears down in it. I'll keep it in the box with this diary. It'll help me cope.*

30th July: *I've been writing in my journal day and night. It's draining but I'm writing poetry and everything I feel. Only two months before it goes to court.*

3rd August: *I went to the police station to identify somebody but I didn't even know who I was looking for. It was horrible. I recognised three men but I didn't know which one it was. When I got home I shut the door and cried.*

29th August: *I met one of the lawyers today. She showed me pages of reports the defence lawyers have about me. They're not relevant to the case but they make my character and personality look bad. I feel exposed.*

14th September: *I know that God will care for me. He'll be proud of me for putting all these years of my life into getting justice for myself and others. He can see the good in me. He can see and feel my courage, strength, determination, my faith and hope. He will let me be free.*

I opened up the pink box containing my journal and packed away my diary for the very last time. I was eighteen years old. It had taken two years for the police to gather the evidence but now the date for the trial was approaching and I was ready.

CHAPTER 24

THE TRIAL

The trial was scheduled to last for six weeks and it would be heard at the Crown Court. I wondered how I would ever get through it.

On the first day, Dad turned up at the house. Even though I wanted to do it alone, he was determined to come with me.

'Cig?' he asked, when he noticed my hands were shaking.

'Yeah,' I smiled.

I wasn't his little girl anymore and he knew it. I was all grown up and now I was even smoking in front of him. These men had ruined my life: they'd made me grow up quicker than I'd ever wanted to. But now, after a two-and-a-half-year investigation, I finally had my day in court.

I'd been assigned a support worker called Karen six months before the trial and she'd been my rock. Over the past few months, she'd regularly popped in to see me. I always showed her what I'd written in my diary – she was one of the few people I trusted. At times, Karen put me before her own family and in many ways became my guardian angel. She gave me strength when I most needed it. In many ways she saved my life.

During the run-up to the trial, my Aunt Sarah offered to take me out for the day. As we walked along, I realised that we'd stumbled into an Asian neighbourhood. Suddenly, I was back in the secret house with faceless men, their hands pawing at my body, hurting me. I started to retch, then I vomited on the floor. My aunt became upset but eventually I managed to pull myself together. However, the fear had been real. I fretted. If I was like this now, how would I ever cope in court with the real thing standing in the dock?

A uniformed police officer picked us up on the morning of the trial and Dad and me travelled with him to the Crown Court. Karen met us there. I didn't want Mum or Phil to go. To be honest, I didn't want anyone there – I felt too embarrassed.

Prior to the trial, I'd had to identify all of the men. Each one had been mixed in with seven other innocent faces and I had to pick them out from the crowd. It wasn't hard. I successfully identified Zeb, Aban, Wadi, Tali, Rafan and Isam. Even so, the police made me watch a CD featuring the men's faces twice because it was a legal requirement.

The other girl, who had been twelve years old when she was abused, was too frightened to testify so the police couldn't make her. They traced another girl who'd been thirteen at the time. She was now fifteen, but her family also refused to let her stand as a witness – I was on my own.

It was decided it'd be best if I gave evidence from a side room via video link. A court usher led me in and the room was empty apart from a chair and a camera, which linked directly back into the court room. They could see me but I couldn't see them. I'd wanted to be strong and look my abusers in the eye but the thought of being in the same room as them made me feel physically sick. In the end, the decision was taken – this would be the best way forward. I couldn't back down now.

I'd been given a tour of the court room prior to the hearing so I knew what it looked like and where everyone sat. Giving evidence via the video link unnerved me because I knew I'd be able to hear everyone in the court room. I would see who was talking to me but thankfully, I wouldn't see Zeb or the others. I wondered if they'd see me. I hated the fact that the jury would be watching my every move. I was worried about whether I'd come across okay and I just prayed that they'd believe me.

When my time came, I took a deep breath and told the truth. Sure enough, my version of events was brought into question, as was my character. The defence teams called me a wild-child – a sexually active troublemaker. They said I was a rebel who hung around outside shops, drinking and smoking. Each one ripped into me and my version of events but I held my nerve as they all but called me a liar.

Then one brought up the fact that I'd been sick in the street when I'd found myself in an Asian neighbourhood. He said I'd been sick because I was racist. The arguments against me were so far-fetched, they were laughable.

Lauren was called to give evidence, which she did via video link over two days. I wasn't allowed to see or speak to her during the trial so I wasn't sure what she'd said. But I later found out she'd told the court about the second house with Rafan. She also told them about Isam and the others from the shop. Lauren didn't know Zeb or anything about the 'secret' house, but she'd just backed up everything else I'd said.

One afternoon, I was sitting in a side room when I was asked to hand over my mobile phone. They were convinced I'd been speaking to Lauren and that I was telling her what to say. It made me angry. At first I refused but I was told the jury would be suspicious if I chose to say no. In the end, I gave them the phone because I had nothing to hide. If I hadn't already felt exposed, I did now. I hated the thought of complete strangers scanning through all my calls and texts. Half an hour later I was given my mobile back. They hadn't found anything but I felt utterly violated.

Soon it was the defendants' turn to take the stand.

Tali denied even knowing me and said we'd never had sex above the shop or in his car. He'd changed jobs and he said he knew Wadi, but denied knowing any of the others. I couldn't believe it.

Rafan admitted having sex with me once but said that as I'd been dressed older than my years, he'd thought I was at least nineteen years old. He said he'd seen me drinking and smoking and had assumed I was older. He admitted lying to the police at first about knowing me because he was married with children and didn't want to be cast out of his community. But how could he think I was nineteen? I'd been wearing my school uniform when we'd first met.

Wadi also protested his innocence. He called me wild and denied giving me cigarettes and alcohol. He also denied that he'd had sex with me. He told the jury that during the investigation I'd continued to pester him, visiting him at his shop. It was a lie. I suggested to his lawyer that if I'd been to the shop, as Wadi had said, they should show the CCTV footage in court. I knew the shop had been fitted with CCTV, so if it was true then surely I'd be caught on camera? The lawyer seemed flustered and later told the court his client had informed him that the camera had been broken on the day in question. I'd just blown Wadi's story out of the water.

Zeb told the jury he'd met me by chance because I'd got hold of his phone number and pestered him. He then said I'd made up false allegations of rape because he'd rebuffed my advances.

The trial progressed as, day by day, I listened to more and more of this nonsense. Finally, halfway through the trial, the jury, on the direction of the judge, found Isam not guilty. I couldn't believe it – I was in total shock. How could he get away scot-free after everything I'd been through? I felt completely gutted.

That night when I returned from court I shut myself in my bedroom. A police officer came to see me but I refused to go to court again. What was the point? If the jury didn't believe me about Isam, then why would they believe me about the others? He'd got away with it, so what was to say the others wouldn't too? The police officer listened and eventually calmed me down. Then he made me see sense; we'd come this far, so I owed it to myself to see it through to the end.

Days later, the jury acquitted Rafan too. I don't know why they found them both not guilty; they were as bad as the others but for some reason the jury chose to believe them and not me.

Doubt plagued me. I wondered if Lauren had painted a rosy picture of Rafan – I knew she'd always fancied him and had even called him her first true love. I wondered if she'd believed him when he told her how much he loved her, just as I'd believed them all.

The thought that both Isam and Rafan were free men hurt me inside. I wanted to take a knife and hunt them down. But it was pointless – then I'd be the one locked away for the rest of my life. They knew what they'd done and now they'd have to live with the guilt for the rest of their lives. Just because they'd walked free didn't mean they were innocent.

After the not guilty verdicts only four were left standing in the dock – Zeb, Aban, Wadi and Tali. The jury retired to consider their verdicts and I sat and waited.

Angela and Karen called me to the police station to make a victim statement in case the men were found guilty. I told them how the abuse had shaped and ruined my childhood – how I'd never be able to claw back those happy years. These men had ruined my entire life so far and they still were. It wouldn't be over until the jury had reached a decision.

Exhausted from bearing my soul for the very last time, I drifted off outside, cigarette in hand, for a moment of quiet reflection. Moments later, Angela came to find me. The jury had returned with the verdicts.

I held my breath.

'They found Aban not guilty,' she said.

My face fell. I knew it – they'd get away with it, the whole lot of them. Why did I even bother? I shook my head in despair.

'What about the others?' I gasped. Then I held my breath, too frightened to know the answer.

'Guilty.'

Guilty.

Tears filled my eyes and started to stream down my cheeks. The jury had believed me, not them. For the first time in years, I felt complete and utter relief. Raising my fist, I punched the air with delight – I couldn't help it. All the waiting, all those months I'd felt suicidal – it was over and I'd been vindicated.

Zeb, Wadi and Tali would be sent to prison, where they'd be

locked away for a total of 22 years. Zeb was handed a twelve-year jail term for raping and sexually abusing me, whilst Wadi was given six years and Tali four.

Sam was due to be separately sentenced as the cases were not deemed to be connected, but at least he had the decency to plead guilty and spare me a second trial. Two months later, Sam – the lad I'd considered my boyfriend – was jailed for two years for nine offences of sexual activity with a child. He'd not been involved with the grooming ring and was said to be genuinely remorseful, but he was still a paedophile and he'd still had sex with a child – and that lost childhood had been mine.

I'd done it. I'd seen both cases through and now these bastards were on the Sex Offenders Register, where they'd be closely monitored and kept away from children. They were marked men and everyone knew who and what they were. Now they were behind bars where they couldn't hurt, abuse or groom another child.

The battle to get to this point had been tough and I was left scarred by my experience. I felt angry because whilst I suffered, the other abusers were out there living a normal life. During the investigation, I'd been shouted at in the street by relatives of those in the dock. I'd been called 'white trash', even a 'prostitute'. Their families tried to intimidate me, tried to get me to back down. But I wouldn't – I needed to do this for the other young victims.

I thought the sentences would bring relief but they brought more anger. These men could have spared me further trauma by admitting their guilt, but they were arrogant and refused. They'd been allowed to intimidate and abuse me all over again, this time in a court of law. Defiant right up to the end, they'd been certain they'd win – but they hadn't.

Slowly the pain lifted. And, as each day passed, I began to feel stronger: I'd got justice.

Zeb and the others didn't think I'd do it. They didn't think I was strong enough to expose them for what they were. I'd always been their victim, but not anymore. I'd got justice not only for myself but for the countless other victims of this vile grooming crime.

These evil men had robbed my childhood from me. They saw me as a sex toy, not a human being. They thought they had all the power, but somehow I discovered an inner strength and fought back. I fought for all those children who weren't strong or brave enough to do so.

Zeb and his friends got what they deserved and if I have one wish, it is this: for someone to torture and intimidate them in the same way they did with me and all those other little girls. I dream someone stronger will overpower them, so that they feel the utter terror I did every single day of my teenage years.

I'd been to hell and back, but now it was finally over. Their lives were over but mine was just beginning.

CHAPTER 25

MOVING ON

O pening up my journal one last time, I grabbed a pen. The pages were bulging with my notes, fears and thoughts over the past few years but this would be my final entry. A poem I'd been carrying inside me came spilling out onto the page. My hand struggled to keep up as the words flowed from deep inside. I began to write.

My Story

A story so haunting, a story cold,
But this is a story that needs to be told.
All those years you made me feel so bad,
All those years when you made me feel so sad.
All those years when I thought I couldn't cope,
I can't believe I still have hope.
You took me into a room and you locked the door,

STOLEN GIRL

You violently pushed me down to the floor.
You overpowered me — I was so helpless,
You hurt me but didn't care — you left me in a mess.
You didn't care when you made me cry,
When you hurt me so much I wanted to die.
Why didn't you stop when I screamed no?
Why didn't you listen or let me go?
I lay curled up and wounded on my bed,
Feeling worthless, nothing, just totally dead.
After all those years I had my say,
Then finally, there came the day.
The day you would all pay.
You thought you controlled me, thought I'd never tell,
But one day I did and I sent you to hell.
Did you really think they would just let you walk away?
Did you think you could have it all your way?
The tables were turned, and I had the power,
Like the cowards you were the court saw you cower.
Every word you said was a lie,
Hearing you say them, I wanted to die.
You ripped me apart,
Inside I had a cold and damaged heart.
The hurt you've caused is beyond repair,
There's so much pain, too much to bear.
You have torn me inside; you have torn my soul,
Sometimes I wonder if I'll ever feel whole.
Writing this poem I have shed many tears,
But I know the end is finally near.
When I feel alone, I just pick up a pen,
I vent out my anger, a message to send.
My writing is the key,

MOVING ON

It unlocks what's buried inside of me.
A story so haunting, a story so cold,
A story that has finally, now been told.

Placing the pink journal back in its box, I pushed down the lid. It was over. The case which had ripped me and my family apart was now dead and buried. It lay rotting inside the hearts of the men who'd done this to me. Now I was moving on.

Today, I'm twenty-one years old and I have a boyfriend called Jack. Unlike the men who abused me, Jack is amazing. He's there for me when life gets me down, which it still does, but he's also there to share the good times too.

We started going out not long after the trial had finished. I met him in a club but we'd known each other at school. He told me he'd fancied me all those years before, when I'd felt so utterly crap – I was astounded. I knew he'd make a difference to my life and he has. Together we are complete. And, when he says he loves me, I believe him because he means it. It's taken me a long time but I have learned how to trust and love again.

Writing the book has given me some sort of closure because it's helped me move on. I've written it because I want to make a difference – I don't want others to suffer as I did.

Grooming is evil, immoral and illegal – it must be stopped. These men target the most vulnerable members of society: our children. We must be there as adults to protect them, but our communities must also work together to stamp out this vile crime.

This act is often carried out by Asian men who primarily target white girls and the number of cases coming to light is on the increase. Thankfully, these predatory men are in the minority. Most Asian men are law-abiding, hard-working and decent. However, there is a small minority who look to target white girls: they believe these girls, by the very colour of their skin, are promiscuous and are there to be used and abused. They are despicable men and they must be stopped and brought to justice by both communities.

My case is just the tip of the iceberg. I fear there are many more children out there like me, who believe these men when they tell them that they love them. They do not: they are paedophiles who groom girls so they can abuse them and pass them around as sexual playthings. These offenders must be caught and dealt with. We need to start talking to one another, breaking down barriers and recognising that this *does* happen. It's the only way we can stop it from blighting the next generation.

I hope that by speaking out, I can help other victims find the strength to come forward to report such crimes. If not, I fear there will be many more just like me.

Despite everything, I'm slowly rebuilding my life. For the first time I'm looking forward to the future because I actually believe I have one. I've wasted enough of my life worrying about what these bastards did to me but now I refuse to waste another minute because they're not worth it. They're behind bars where they belong – where they can never hurt another little girl again.

I feel proud of myself that I've found the strength to speak out: I know I have done the right thing.